THE THEATRE
THROUGH ITS STAGE DOOR

David Belasco as He Appears To-day

The Theatre Through Its Stage Door

By *David Belasco*

Edited by
LOUIS V. DEFOE

BENJAMIN BLOM   New York/London

First Published 1919
Reissued 1969 by
Benjamin Blom, Inc., Bronx, New York 10452
and 56 Doughty Street, London, W.C. 1

Library of Congress Catalog Card Number 69-56534

Printed in the United States of America

93538

CONTENTS

93538

ILLUSTRATIONS

ILLUSTRATIONS

A FOREWORD

THE chapters in this book are the result of occasional leisure hours extending over the past two years. They have been suggested by what is, I believe, the experience of others who, like myself, have been closely identified during a long period with the artistic direction of the dramatic stage.

Because it does not seek aid in the form of government subsidy or millionaire endowment, the theatre in the United States, as in England, is regarded as a private enterprise. But when the theatre is rightly conducted it must acknowledge grave public duties and responsibilities which, I think, are now recognized by those among its workers who rightly understand it as an art and strive to serve its esthetic purposes. They are members of a public, or at least a quasi-public, profession. However sincere may be their desire for privacy, they are, in a sense, public personages to whom other persons assume the right—and also should be accorded the right—to come for information or advice.

In one of the following pages I have said that "the observation and experience of those of

us who are within the theatre lead to the conclusion that nearly every one is not only a playgoer, but, at one time or another, aspires to
write or even tries to write a play." I might
add without much exaggeration that many who
do not come within this category are seized, at
some time in their lives, with the temptation
to become actors. The mimetic impulse is
strong and it is almost universal in human
nature, though it asserts itself in various forms.

At any rate, it cannot be denied that the
profession of the theatre appeals powerfully
and romantically to the public, especially to
the youthful part of the public. Happily, it
is to the decided advantage of the theatre that
it exerts this attraction. A lively interest in
the stage, its art, its work, and its people, if
it does not always result in breeding playwrights and players, breeds playgoers; and
it is through an ardor for playgoing, which has
become one of our national traits, that the
theatre advances and prospers.

From people in every part of this country,
with aspirations or fancied aspirations to enter
one or another of the branches of the stage
profession, comes a very large part of the
voluminous correspondence which daily reach-
es my theatre. To these thousands of letters
asking information or counsel on a great va-
riety of subjects related to my profession I
aim always to reply. Necessarily my answers

must be brief. For the most part they consist, unfortunately, of a few words of disillusionment to their senders, who, in nine cases out of ten, know nothing of the theatre from its inside.

The same attention I cannot observe, to my regret, in the cases of the many daily callers who seek interviews at my studio. My engagements and my limited leisure do not permit the courtesy I would prefer to show even to those visitors who are personally unknown to me. But long experience has made me familiar with the questions which they, and also the great majority of my correspondents, are most likely to ask, so it was as a general reply to those seekers after information or guidance regarding the theatre, its art and its requirements, that I undertook the opening chapters in this volume, which bears the title, *The Theatre Through Its Stage Door*—the door through which the great public cannot peer into it.

Those first candid observations were published in *The Ladies' Home Journal*. If I had hoped that they would decrease the number of letters and visits from people interested in the theatre either as a vocation or as a source of entertainment, I was mistaken, for they prompted an increased flood. Accordingly, the succeeding chapters which compose this book resulted. But I did not have at my disposal the time necessary to put them in the completed state that they required, and I make acknowledgment to Louis V. De Foe, who throughout twenty years, as Dramatic Critic of *The New York World*, has been my intimate and helpful friend, for editing and revising them, and also for rearranging them as they appear in this volume. Not all its contents has been published before, though certain chapters have appeared in *The Saturday Evening Post*, *The Ladies' Home Journal*, and *Munsey's Magazine*.

I have attempted to epitomize my theories, views, and practices in the making of my dramatic productions, in the training and development of my actors, and in the regulation and direction of the manifold elements which enter into the mounting and unfolding of every work of dramatic art, not as a treatise on these different subjects, but as information for the many who, I know by experience, are curious to learn of the work of the theatre through other sources than the proscenium opening.

Especially have I endeavored to warn the aspirants to a career in the theatre of what energy, devotion, and sacrifice will be demanded of them if they expect to win even ordinary success—or what passes for success— in the profession of the stage.

The theatre of my conception is the noblest of the arts—noblest and most influential because it is, of all the arts, the most democratic and closest to the hearts and lives of the people. He who is ambitious to reach a high place among the workers within its walls must be prepared to give to it the best that is in him of unremitting labor and unselfishness.

DAVID BELASCO.

January, 1919.

THE THEATRE
THROUGH ITS STAGE DOOR

THE THEATRE
THROUGH ITS STAGE DOOR

Chapter I

I

COULD only the outer world look in upon the little, mysterious inner world of the theatre from under the dim lantern which hangs over the stage door, instead of from beneath the glittering electric lights over the front entrance, there would soon be a decrease in the never-ending but always-changing rows of eager young men and women who daily line the walls of the waiting-room outside the office of every dramatic producer and manager.

If more were known of the difficult road which winds up-hill from its obscure beginning to the place in the theatre's sun, which is the limelight, the steady flood of letters from unknown people in every station of life, each with its plea which constant repetition has made so familiar, would presently diminish.

Here is an example of thousands of such letters sent to the Belasco Theatre every year.

It is postmarked from a small town in Illinois, the name of which I have never heard before. It is written in a prim hand and composed with evident care. I can guess the heart-throbs between its lines, for I recall a time when I gave whole days to writing similar letters, and I remember the mingled hopes and misgivings I poured into them.

I am a girl eighteen years old, of fairly good appearance, I should say, with brown eyes and hair. I have finished school, and while my people are fairly well-to-do, I feel I ought to enter some profession and learn to support myself.

From the time I was a child I have loved the theatre. Nothing else has ever interested me nearly so much. I think I have some real talent for the stage—that is, my family and all my friends tell me I have. I have acted in several amateur plays in our city and have even had some of the most important parts. I have always received much applause.

After thinking it over carefully I am writing you to ask if you can find a chance for me in any of your companies. I can even come to New York to see you if you think there is any hope. I would prefer to act serious parts because I believe I have emotional ability. I would not expect to do very prominent work during the first year or two, so I would not ask very much pay at the start. Will you please consider my application, for it means so much to me?

> Yours very truly,
> AGNES ANDERSON.

An Anderson. But another Mary? I doubt. Yet still I wonder.

If I could give the time to answer fully this letter from my unknown correspondent who evidently has no knowledge whatever of the profession she seems to be so eager to enter I would tell her what I am about to set down in these pages. Her ambition is perfectly legitimate and I do not underestimate the compliment she pays me in asking for my help. In order to carry on the artistic enterprises of the theatre it is necessary that the profession of the stage should attract to itself people from everywhere, and more people, and still more people. The hopeful beginner of to-day may become the famous actor of the years to come. Every one who is possessed of an honest desire to enter an art or trade has the right to ask at least a chance. If those in control of the theatre placed only discouragement in the way of all who are ambitious to come into it, it would stagnate and gradually the most democratic of the arts would disappear.

But there is this to be said in the case of those who aspire to enter the profession of the actor. The thing which makes the theatre so treacherous in its allurement, through no real fault of the theatre itself, is that so many times the novice is attracted to it by its superficial and misleading glamour, rather than because of the real inducements which a career in it offers.

I do not mean that the acting profession is

[3]

not in every sense honorable or that the person who enters it seriously and follows it faithfully and diligently will not find in it satisfaction, happiness, and pecuniary reward. No greater advantages than these three things are to be gained from any other of the arts. What I do mean is that, when seen only from the public's side of the footlights and without real knowledge of the demands placed upon its people, few even so much as surmise at what price of work, persistence, energy, disappointment, and self-sacrifice adequate success in the actor's profession is won.

Almost everything becomes more attractive when viewed from a distance. This is true of every art and profession. It is right that the theatre, especially, should present an outward show of glamour and romance, and that the small part of the player's work which the public sees should seem to be accomplished without effort. People go to the theatre in search of relaxation and pleasure, and these ends the stage can satisfy only under conditions of perfect harmony and ease. So the figures in its mimic life must reveal themselves always in an attractive and enviable light. When the picture through the proscenium opening is not alluring, when its make-believe betrays the effort by which the illusion is created—then the theatre fails to accomplish its most important purpose.

The public—fortunately for itself—prefers not to distinguish between the theatre's completed task and the effort required to bring about its seemingly effortless accomplishment. It never stops to consider that what is so pleasurable and restful, or so absorbing and exciting—and so apparently spontaneous—is achieved only through infinite preparation, calculation, study, and experience, through the unromantic nerve- and body-wearing toil of weeks of preliminary, and afterward, daily rehearsal by those behind the curtain.

It does not reflect that the actor is continually under the scrutiny of his audience, that he must constantly appear at his best, even when he feels at his worst, that he himself is the canvas on which he paints the picture of his character, and that the canvas and the picture he paints, in order to satisfy, must be flawless. Here lies at once the art and deception of the theatre—a profession in which sauce for the goose is never sauce for the gander.

The experience of a score of years as a producer of plays and director of theatres convinces me that not one out of five hundred, either women or men, who yield to the impulse to attempt a career in the theatre even so much as surmises what will be demanded and what must be given to win unfavored success. Yet I always hesitate to discourage the applicants who come to me for advice or assistance, even when at first observation they seem to be unsuited for the work they are anxious to attempt. I always reflect that a hasty, ill-considered word may rob the theatre, which needs them so much, of a future Modjeska, Clara Morris, or Mrs. Carter; of a Jefferson, Mansfield, or David Warfield.

At such times I recall an incident which happened while I was preparing to produce "Zaza" in 1899. One day a Brooklyn girl about sixteen years old came to me with the familiar story. She was tall, thin, angular, very awkward, not at all prepossessing, and her face was spotted with freckles. She said her name was Ruth Dennis and that she was poor.

"I want to do something on the stage," she told me. "I know I am not graceful, but I can dance a little. I want to be an actress and I think I have ability. I will do anything to get a start. Can't you help me?"

At first glance she appeared to be entirely unsuited for the work on which she had set her heart. Her frank admission of inexperience showed me she was especially unfitted for anything I might have to offer. But as I studied the mobile lines in her face and the changing light in her eyes I was struck by the undeveloped possibilities in the girl. I asked her to go through a few steps and discovered that she had original talent. I introduced a

[6]

little dance into "Zaza," a very trivial bit, and engaged her for the part of Alice.

Once in my theatre, the energy and ambition of this girl had no limit. The audiences liked her dance, and this recognition greatly encouraged her. Soon she came to me and said she had no place to practise while not at actual rehearsals. I told her she could have my stage whenever it was not in use. Every morning after that she came to my old Republic Theatre and practised alone. I never saw a girl with such a keen desire to succeed.

When it came time to take the "Zaza" company to London, she asked me if she could not go along, although the salary was small. She said she wanted to study the dancers in Europe and hoped to save enough money to enable her to spend a few days in Paris. While we were in London I would frequently excuse her from a performance so she might go to another theatre and watch some dancer of especial note. By great economy she also saved enough money for her cherished Paris trip. And meanwhile, whenever I happened in at the theatre during the day, I found her on the stage practising interminably and always alone.

When I made my "Du Barry" production a few years later I gave her a part and also a solo dance. By that time she had improved so much that audiences always gave her an encore which I was obliged to grant, much as I disliked to, for it interrupted the continuity of the play. She had then changed her name to Ruth St. Denis. I saw that dancing was her most natural medium of artistic expression, and advised her to give up thought of becoming an actress and devote all her energy to the dance.

It was hard for her to put away the idea of acting, but she finally agreed that I was right, and when the run of "Du Barry" ended we parted company. A little later she came to me and said she had composed a symbolical dance and wanted me to see her perform it. She had bought her costumes out of her savings, and friends who had become interested in her work had provided the scenery. That was the "Radia" dance which brought Ruth St. Denis her first substantial prestige as an independent artist.

She is one of the best examples I have ever known of a self-taught woman. Her career is proof of the chance which is open to every woman in the theatre, provided she has ability, an honest desire to succeed, and the patience and perseverance necessary to win recognition. Ruth St. Denis turned out to be a dancer instead of an actress, but with any such girl as she the result would have been the same, no matter which of the two arts she had followed.

Among the crowds which besiege the offices of dramatic producers there is seldom a candidate with the stamina and determination of this Brooklyn girl who at the outset had every physical disadvantage to contend against. But they are not, as is so generally believed, all romantic, stage-struck young girls and indolent young men. From my talks with many hundreds of them, and from reading their thousands of appealing letters, I have come to the conclusion that in a great majority of cases they look upon the theatre either as a refuge or the "easiest way." Many of them are victims, or at least think they are victims, of the big and little tragedies of life.

Both men and women who have failed in the other professions because of unfitness, laziness, or lack of the faculty of application, turn to the stage as a last resort. They do not understand that they are then courting the most exacting and difficult profession of all. These people cannot realize that the deficiencies in themselves which brought about their previous failures are almost sure to be intensified if they try to become actors. Among them are young lawyers grown tired of prosaic briefs, young doctors whose fees have been too slender or too slow, and even ministers whose emotional tendencies have outgrown the limitations of their pulpits.

A successful play which happens to contain an attractive character in any of these professions—I might give, as examples, the young physician and trained nurse in my production of "The Boomerang"—will persuade many who belong actually to such professions that they could have played the rôle just as well. But to be a holy man, for instance, and to compel a theatre audience to believe you are a holy man, are two quite different things.

Domestic difficulty drives many restless women to the stage door of the theatre. They turn to it impulsively as a refuge from discontent. Occasionally I have run across one among them whose ambition has not been mistaken, for suffering is the hard school which develops the deeper emotions in men and women. I do not mean to confuse these unfortunates with the victims of divorce courts who seek to commercialize notoriety by exhibiting themselves in public places. The standard of the dramatic profession has improved so much in late years that it now discourages such sensationalism.

Success, or what seems to be success, in amateur theatricals also yields the theatre an abundant harvest—those who mistake the kindly applause of their friends as proof that they have the acting gift. The awakening in store for them, when they are judged by the rigid standards of the professional stage, is bitter. Yet from among these emerges now and then a Mrs. Langtry or a Mrs. Patrick Campbell.

Vanity is one of the commonest of the weak-

Entrance to David Belasco's Studio Above the Belasco Theatre

The studio contains seven rooms filled with books, antiques, and curios

David Belasco Giving Stage Directions to Frances Starr in
a Rehearsal During the Run of "Marie-Odile"

nesses which lead people to believe they are born to act. A handsome face and a fine physique are worthless in the theatre if they are expressionless. The pride of doting parents whose children have won prizes for reciting well in school is another thing which helps to keep filled the waiting line at the stage door. Among them may be the occasional potential Julia Marlowe. But no child should be forced into a theatrical career merely because it is precocious.

I have always found the humbler byways of life the stage's best recruiting-ground. The shop-girl, the milliner, the girl in any vocation which serves as a school of experience, will be better equipped, if she also has fair intelligence and ability, for a career in the theatre than the society girl who is the graduate of a finishing-school. Drawing-room manners never bring as much to the stage as the unconscious manners of the girl in whom grace is born. One has grace God-given; the other has grace acquired. I can deck my stage much better with girls from the milliner shops than from the schools where polite deportment is taught.

I do not mean that education is not a valuable aid to a career in the theatre. But the education gained from books, beyond the fact that it sharpens the mental faculties, is not indispensable. It is significant—and no less true of the present than of the past—that our greatest artists of the stage have been self-taught. I have never seen men or women born with gold spoons in their mouths bring much to the stage. The great actors all came into the theatre humbly and remained humble, without false ideas that its life is easy or that its rewards can be quickly gained, and they came always out of instinctive love for its art.

II

Throughout its history it has been one of the unfailing sources of the theatre's power and influence that it is the melting-pot to which all kinds of people from all classes come. Among all the arts, the drama is the most democratic and cosmopolitan. So the theatre must appeal to every taste and it must reflect all kinds of life if it is to command that universal interest which is essential to it. This end can be better accomplished—indeed, it can only be accomplished—when the workers within its walls are themselves a cosmopolitan band, without class distinctions and welded into one body in which all stand on the same level.

In choosing the beginners who afterward have become successful in my theatres I have never paid much attention to physical qualifications. What I have demanded principally are youth and temperament. It is possible always

to train the voice.   Physical imperfections can
usually be corrected.   Yet thousands have applied to me in the belief that with a pretty
face and figure they have already won half the
battle.

A very ordinary face may become beautiful
under the emotions of life, whether of happiness
or of sorrow, and often the most beautiful faces
show very little emotion, whether in life or
in the theatre.

Lack of beauty has not barred the way to
fame for the most renowned women of the stage.
Rachel, Charlotte Cushman, Janauschek, Bernhardt, Duse, Clara Morris, and Mrs. Leslie
Carter, among the great emotional actresses,
were not beautiful women.   Adelaide Neilson
was, though she is about the only one I can
recall.   Among the comédiennes Ellen Terry
and Ada Rehan reminded me of butterflies.
They were charming, but they were not beautiful.   If either had been only beautiful, she
would have had no face to glow.

It has been the same with the theatre's great
actors.   Kean, McCullough, Forrest, Salvini,
Coquelin, Mansfield, and Forbes-Robertson
were not handsome men, but to what heights
they arose!   David Warfield, with his homely,
expressive face, makes a deeper and truer appeal to women than all the Adonises of the
stage put together.

It was her ability to express vividly, in a face

that was not beautiful, the emotions she felt which convinced me, before I had ever seen her attempt to act, that Mrs. Leslie Carter was destined to a successful career. When she first came to my attention she had had no training for the stage, though as a young girl she had appeared in a number of school plays. She was bent upon becoming an actress, but she expected to begin at the top. She did not have the slightest notion of what is demanded for a successful career on the stage. When I told her that to drill her would require years of hard work, her ardor cooled so perceptibly that I left her without any thought of developing her.

But the next time we met her attitude had undergone a great change. She was then in the midst of domestic difficulties. The theatre was no longer a plaything to her, but a means of earning a living. I was at that time —in the late 'eighties—in a secluded place in the country, hard at work with William C. De Mille on the writing of "The Charity Ball," and we had directed that our whereabouts be kept unknown.

Nevertheless, Mrs. Carter found me out and caught me unawares. She fairly overwhelmed me with tears and entreaties. I did the best I could to make plausible excuses, explaining that the play Mr. De Mille and I were writing for the Lyceum Theatre Company required all my time. There she sat, with eyes fixed upon me which expressed more than her torrents of words. As she begged my assistance her voice and face grew eloquent, and when she began to tell of her domestic troubles her manner became almost tragic. Nothing about her was beautiful or even pretty, but the radiance of her features, the eloquence of her soul, and the magnetism of her highly keyed, temperamental nature convinced me then and there that she would go far, if only her natural abilities could be developed and controlled.

To completely assure myself, I told her to memorize emotional scenes from certain standard plays, and I returned to New York to hear her recite them. Standing on the stage before me, her natural grace entirely left her and she became rigidly self-conscious and awkward. It was plain that she must undergo much training and development, though the instinct to act and the ability to express emotions she felt were still there. There was always, too, her dogged desire to succeed.

So we went to work together. One deficiency after another was detected and corrected. I have never seen a more tireless or persistent worker. By the end of another year she was ready to appear in "The Ugly Duckling" and conquer, by the sheer strength of her natural acting, a public which at first was inclined to be hostile toward her. The prestige which Mrs.

Carter afterward gained as the emotional heroines in "The Heart of Maryland," "Zaza," "Du Barry," and "Adrea" every one knows. The secret of her success was willingness to work and pluck, plus the imagination and natural talent she brought with her into the theatre.

Mrs. Carter's career is exceptional in our theatres. She is one of the few examples I know of women who have begun at the top, yet have succeeded. Another such example is furnished by the comparatively short but brilliant career of Mary Anderson. What both of these women have done, each in her own way, would be folly for almost any one else to attempt to follow. They illustrate, however, what may be accomplished in the theatre through determination, labor, and perseverance.

The possibility of succeeding on the stage in spite of seemingly physical disqualification is no better proved than by Robert Taber's triumph over a deformity which thousands who have seen him act must have failed to detect. A good many years ago, when I was associated with Franklin Sargent's dramatic school, a young man came to ask if I thought it possible for him to become an actor. He walked with a limp, for one of his legs had become shortened from an illness he had suffered in childhood. The heavy-soled shoe he wore did not correct the deformity, and one of his shoulders drooped below the level of the other. His general appearance was that of an invalid. But the earnestness of his appeal awakened my interest. I asked him to read for me, and the scenes from some of Shakespeare's plays, which he had at his tongue's end, soon led me to see that he had the spark of genius.

I explained the physical disadvantages which stood in the way of his ambition, but told him that with patient endeavor it might be possible to overcome them. A routine of calisthenic exercises was prescribed for him and he followed it faithfully through an entire year. His body began to strengthen slowly, he gradually acquired grace and poise. I advised him to have a surgical shoe made with the inner sole raised so that his shortened leg would not be noticed. Meanwhile his poetic nature deepened, his romantic style broadened, and the promise I had at first detected in him began to develop.

As leading actor for Julia Marlowe, whom he afterward married, Robert Taber became one of the most finished and magnetic actors in romantic characters of his day. He went to England and won even greater success in Henry Irving's company. But his physical frailty could not endure the trying life of the theatre. He died when still a young man. He is another example of what iron determination can achieve for those who enter the profession of the theatre with honest motives.

Even age need not be a bar to ultimate success on the stage, although, since I prefer to train, myself, the people who appear in my plays, I am always inclined to scrutinize applicants for theatrical positions with reference to their youth. Some actors do not "find themselves" until comparatively late in their careers. There is the case of David Warfield. My association with him, which resulted in his turning to serious rôles, did not begin until he had already won notable success as an impersonator of humorous, eccentric types in the uproarious field of burlesque and musical comedy.

When I returned to New York in 1900, after presenting Mrs. Carter in London in "Zaza," I decided to add an emotional male actor to my list of stars. Mrs. Carter was then approaching her zenith in pyrotechnical characters, and Blanche Bates, another young star, was very popular in plays which breathed the buoyancy and freedom of out-of-door life. But I had no distinguished man on whom I could rely for a certain kind of plays I was anxious to produce.

I, of course, had known Warfield. He came, originally, from San Francisco, my native city. The first time I ever saw him he was standing on a soap-box, reciting verses to a street crowd. He afterward became an impersonator of Hebrew types in various companies, and finally joined Weber and Fields's burlesque organization, which was then in its heyday. I recalled how once, in a broad burlesque of Annie Russell's "Catherine," I had observed an uproarious audience quiet down to serious attention under the influence of his wistful expression and the curious note of pathos in his voice.

Mr. Warfield was then appearing in "Barbara Fidgety," a travesty of Julia Marlowe's play, "Barbara Frietchie," which Clyde Fitch wrote. At the music-hall one night I again noted his peculiar influence over the audience in a mock-pathetic episode in the piece. It occurred to me instantly that in him lay the greatest potentialities as an emotional star. When we joined our artistic fortunes a season later my selection of him was received generally with derision.

Other managers could not imagine Warfield as anything but a comic actor. But two characters, Anton Von Barwig, in "The Music Master," and Peter Grimm, in "The Return of Peter Grimm," have proved how great was the genius that had been stifled up to that time.

So age, though it is one of the most sinister enemies to the actor's art, cannot actually defeat his ambition. If great ability in hidden lines be born in him, it must some day make itself known.

The special ability and honest desire to succeed which have brought to fame these exceptional men and women to whom I have referred I, of course, do not expect to find even in a very small minority of the applicants who come knocking at the stage door of the theatre or who send me their letters burdened with stories of hopes and ambitions. The great majority of them, I find, have yielded to passing impulse or have entirely mistaken what they think is the mission which nature intended for them.

Nevertheless, as I always have a number of plays in preparation, I must ever be on the lookout for chance talent. I make it a point to see as many would-be actors as my time permits. It does not take very long for me to gain a fairly accurate idea of their motives and possibilities. I allow them to talk, and meanwhile I note the quality of their voices and watch the expression of their faces. If they feel character at all—that is, if they have temperament—I can invariably tell whether it is comic, emotional, or tragic.

I cross-examine them in an effort to surprise them, and if I find they are pliable and quick at grasping and expressing a suggested mood, I endeavor to interest myself in them. They may become useful to me, even if I have nothing in prospect for them at the moment.

The theatrical profession, like the others, is crowded, but there is room in it for all. I have sometimes talked to a hundred fairly experienced actors and actresses, looked through the casts of all the current plays, and ransacked the small stock companies and vaudeville houses in a search for a person with peculiar qualifications needed for a rôle I may have in mind, and then have blundered upon just the right person in some complete stranger among the applicants in my waiting-room.

Next to ability I look for sincerity in the people I take into my companies. If I give my time to developing and rehearsing them for parts, however small, I must feel that I can depend upon them absolutely. Like all other producers, I have sometimes been a victim of ingratitude, which is my synonym for the so-called "artistic temperament"; but usually my confidence has not been misplaced.

The enviable place which Frances Starr holds in the affections of a great public is the best illustration I can furnish of the advantages which may come to a young player from having won the complete confidence of her manager. She is about the best example I can recall of an actress in whom are combined the five all-important factors—ability, imagination, industry, patience, and loyalty.

I was on the lookout, as usual, for talent for my stage, when one night, a number of years ago, I happened to visit a modest stock company in New York. At once my attention was attracted by an alert young girl with a finely formed, expressive face and pretty, girlish figure. I noticed the peculiar effect of her charm upon the audience the moment she came on the stage. Reference to the program told me she was Miss Starr.

There was no place for her in any of my plays at that time, but a season or two later, when I needed a new actress for the rôle of Helen Stanton in "The Music Master," I searched again for this young girl who had impressed me so favorably at first sight. I found her in a comedy called "Gallops," and I went again to see her perform. In one scene the changing incidents of a horse-race had to be made known to the audience by the exclamations of an excited party on top of a coach. Miss Starr, who was impersonating the heroine whose lover had staked his all on the result of the race, stood below them on the step of the coach. It was her business to impress her hopes and fears in pantomime. She did not speak a word throughout the scene, but so perfectly did her face indicate every emotion she was supposed to feel that I realized much more clearly than before how great must be her imaginative faculty and sensitiveness. That night I sent word to her to come to see me next day.

Long before I arrived at my office next morning Miss Starr was there. I saw at once that she was eager and determined to get ahead. When I told her I could use her she was willing to sign a contract at once, irrespective of the part I might put her in; but I advised her not to be impulsive, but to consider the matter carefully until the following day. I wanted her to be sure she would not change her mind, for I knew that other managers could offer her better terms at the moment than I.

The contract, signed, came back to me next day. A long time afterward Miss Starr told me she had stopped on her way home that same morning and put her name to it. From that hour her loyalty to me has been absolute and her effort to meet every demand I have placed on her has been indomitable. Such fidelity to my interests I could not fail to appreciate and reward.

Long before the end of "The Music Master" tour I had begun to look for a play containing a suitable and better part for her. Her graceful bearing, lithe figure, arched neck and dark, dancing eyes suggested that she might play a Spanish character well. How "The Rose of the Rancho," which Richard Walton Tully had originally written under the title of "Juanita," was changed to suit the needs of this young actress I shall describe in another chapter. When I came to produce the play I found that every estimate I had made of Miss Starr had been correct, for it quickly set her among the stars. Since then, the salary I paid her in the beginning has been doubled, redoubled, and doubled again, and this, too, without so much as a scratch of a pen between us. No written agreement is necessary to make me absolutely certain of Miss Starr's willingness to attempt whatever I may ask of her.

Other actresses, if they had been cast in the long succession of unsympathetic characters in which I have placed Miss Starr, would surely have been lured away by the tempting offers and promises which other managers and the "movie" manufacturers have made to her. Her head has never been turned by them. Success has never affected her industry or loyalty. Her versatility has expanded, her artistic strength has increased, and she has gone forward, winning the affection of an ever-increasing public, until now, in her own right, she occupies a place in the native theatre which might well be the envy of any actress. I could afford to give all my energy in her behalf, for I have been positive all along that our artistic partnership would be permanent.

III

It has been my experience that where one actor or actress goes ahead in the theatre, gaining that coveted asset, the public's interest and affection, a hundred others will fail, even though they may have great potential ability.

Men and women alike, they cannot stand

applause. It is amazing what vanity, indolence, and cocksureness a little passing adulation will breed even in comparative beginners on the stage. They do not stop to consider how much they owe to the weeks of constant rehearsal by which they are taught to speak their lines as parrots learn to talk, or to the chance opportunity of some lucky little scrap of brilliant dialogue which any other person might have spoken just as well. Indiscriminate, complimentary criticism in the press puffs them up and the deluded creatures even begin to take seriously the laudatory paragraphs sent out about them by the press agent. Soon they become the insufferable victims of that self-satisfaction which is the greatest danger that menaces the actor.

Then, again, there are conditions peculiar to the dramatic profession which are a constant temptation to indolence and which only those with the strongest wills can resist. When a play becomes established for a long run in a large city or starts out on an extended tour, the actors necessarily have a good deal of unoccupied time on their hands. If they belonged to any other of the artistic professions than the stage they would realize that they must utilize such opportunities for study. The painter must learn to mix his colors and cultivate his eye and hand by constant practice. The sculptor must learn to use his tools. The writer must write and revise through solitary hours of grinding labor.

But the young actor quickly gets an idea that if only he brings his body into the theatre he has done his full duty. He thinks all that is necessary is to walk out on the stage, strut for three hours, bow to the audience, and then get away as soon as possible. It never occurs to him that he ought to work eight or ten hours a day, the same as people who follow the other professions—that this is what he is paid to do.

Going through the same part night after night, for months, perhaps, saps his ambition, and if the part he is playing is popular and the audiences applaud, it swells his self-contentment. So he is soon idling away in clubs and restaurants the night hours after the performance which should be devoted to sleep. He lies abed half the day when he ought to be improving himself physically and mentally. He may keep his morals beyond reproach, but he is cultivating an attitude toward life and his profession which in the end means certain disaster to the fine hopes he had when he first decided to become an actor.

When young actors and actresses are setting out on their careers, especially if they are beginning to make progress, it is also hard for them to resist well-meant social attentions. They become, at once, public personages, in a way. The young painter or sculptor, on the other hand, may work for years without personally being sought after by others. The beautiful young actress with charm of manner is always wanted at teas and parties and dances, and the equally engaging young actor finds a swarm of sentimental women flocking after him to decorate their drawing-rooms.

It is hard, of course, for them to deny themselves these pleasant diversions, but all such things consume precious time and, more precious still, the energy which should be devoted to the theatre and their work. Soon you find them accepting rôles which are only types and therefore can be acted without the expense of real effort or the exercise of real ability. Meanwhile the time of youth, the actor's golden opportunity, is slipping away. Before the awakening comes, if it ever does, his chance is gone.

If substantial and permanent success is to come to any player, it will be gained only by subordinating all social pleasures and personal convenience to persistent work. Of the scores, maybe hundreds, to whose stories of ambition I have listened and taken into my companies, only those who have appreciated this fact from the beginning have arrived anywhere in the profession. But the progress of these few has been almost invariable. Some may not have made brilliant names for themselves; great distinction in any artistic calling is in store only for the exceptional small minority. The honest workers, however, have given good accounts of themselves. They have found that the theatre can provide a congenial, satisfactory career and they have been rewarded with popularity, prosperity, and happiness.

But they have also found the theatre to be the hardest of taskmasters. Every hour in the day something can be done for self-improvement, for the time devoted to the actor's appearance before an audience should be a comparatively insignificant part of his day's work. Great help may be gained from rehearsals, not only by going through the part he is to play, but in watching the training of all the others.

In every company is a man or woman of wide experience and fine gifts whose methods may be profitably studied. Having seen these accomplish a striking bit of impersonation and having heard the instructions of the stage director, the beginner who expects sometime to act as well should go to his home or lodging and try to reach the same results himself. For the best place to learn the art of the theatre is the theatre. I have always had a good opinion of dramatic schools, if the instruction is competent, but it is only on the practical stage that real experience is gained. An actor might spend half his life in a dramatic academy and yet fail dismally when he appears before a real audience.

There would be quick improvement in our acting art if the younger members of the profession spent the money for vocal instruction that they waste on pretty hats and frocks. A change for the better would soon come if the time that is frittered away in idleness, social pleasures, and dissipation were devoted to healthful physical exercise in the open air.

The actor ought to expect to study as much as the people of the other professions. He should learn fencing, dancing, and singing, acquire a knowledge of the languages, and read standard literature, both narrative and dramatic. He should accustom himself to observe constantly the life around him, for those whose profession is to interpret life must have an understanding of human nature. Life and character can be studied at any time, in any street-car, or in any crowd. There is a lesson to be learned on every avenue and in every slum.

Above all, young actors should go to the theatre and opera as frequently as they possibly can and become acquainted not only with the work of the successful members of the profession, but with the failures in it as well. It is amazing what one can learn not to do by watching a bad actor struggling with his rôle.

When the actor who is really anxious to succeed follows rigorously such a course as this, he will be prepared when the golden hour strikes. Richard Mansfield's case aptly shows what I mean. He was not well equipped for the stage. Stature, voice, rigidity of manner, ungainly carriage, and defective eyesight—all these stood against him. He had, though, inherited a sensitive artistic temperament and love of music from his mother, who was a great singer. But Mansfield was a student who kept by himself and refused to waste his time. While others disliked him as uncompanionable and mistook the motive of his uncongenial habits, he was really getting ready.

Eventually Mansfield applied for and was given a position in the famous old Union Square Stock Company. Until that time he had done nothing of much promise in the legitimate theatre. A. M. Palmer, the alert manager of the Union Square, and a good judge of men, was aware of his possibilities. In 1883 a production of a translation of Octave Feuillet's play, "A Parisian Romance," was in preparation, when J. H. Stoddart, the leading actor at the Union Square, became dissatisfied with the rôle of Baron Chevrial, for which he had been cast, and threw it down, declining emphatically to appear in it both as unsuitable to him and unworthy of his abilities.

Palmer at once turned the part over to Mansfield, who had been rehearsing up to that time for the trivial character of a young French swell. What happened on the night of January 11, 1883, is a matter of theatrical history. Mansfield brought a thousand adroit and unexpected touches to the rôle of Baron Chevrial which had promised to bring nothing to him. This performance resulted in one of the most surprising successes which our stage has known, and the next morning he awoke to find himself well started on the road to fame. I do not think that Mansfield, during his spectacular career, accomplished really great things for the theatre. But he was tireless in his industry and he always did little things in a big way.

Far back in the days of "The Highest Bidder" and "The Prisoner of Zenda" there was no actor in greater social demand in New York than E. H. Sothern. The adulation he received from the feminine matinée crowd was enough to turn completely the head of any star. Yet Sothern resolutely avoided his silly worshipers and kept at his books. He knew the days of the matinée idol are numbered. His tastes were in the direction of classic drama, and he diligently studied his Shakespeare. When maturer years came and other matinée idols arose in his place, he was prepared to begin his creditable career as an actor of the greatest poetic rôles in English dramatic literature.

The lonely life of the student is only one of many things which any player who resolves to climb must expect to give to the theatre. A career on the stage means a nomadic existence, whether he is successful or not. So in the veins of the actor should always flow a few drops of gipsy blood. He is not a citizen of a definite locality, but a wanderer among many places.

The necessity of almost constant travel is one of the unavoidable hardships which the theatre imposes, and at the same time one of its destructive influences. The people in other professions may become fixed members of the community of their choice, where they may establish permanent homes and regulate the conditions of domestic life. Then they become in a measure responsible to the people around them, which exercises a restraining influence upon conduct. The actor, no matter how pronounced may be his success, cannot expect to confine his work to a single stage. The play must go everywhere. The greater its success the longer the stretches of travel over which it leads its company.

So the actor cannot expect to settle down in the real sense of the term, and he must forgo many of the advantages and comforts of a retired domestic life. Matrimony in his case, therefore, becomes always a dangerous experiment.

I do not mean that there are not happy marriages among the people of the stage. There are plenty of them. But in spite of the proverb, absence does not always tend to make the heart grow fonder, and in the theatre separations of the members of the domestic household for long periods are inevitable.

It is not well for an ambitious young actress to encumber herself with a sweetheart or a husband, especially in the early period of her career. She will go farther if she travels alone, for no woman can be the mistress of a home or the mother of a family and at the same time devote the time and attention to work in the theatre which success demands. Eventually she will find herself relinquishing one in favor of the other, and at this point disaster threatens. Besides, if the husband she takes happens to be an actor, which is of course likely, there is always the danger of artistic rivalry, with its almost certain aftermath of jealousy. There cannot be two geniuses in one family, if perfect peace is to reign.

Whether marriage dilutes the romantic interest which the public takes in its stage favorites is always an open question. That may depend somewhat upon the kind of plays in which the actor or actress appears. Yet I would advise the player of either sex whose professional ambitions are strong to avoid alliances of any kind that tend to divide the affections.

There are compensations in a successful theatrical career for the domestic self-sacrifice it exacts. In no other calling is merit so quickly detected or so richly rewarded—or, alas! so soon forgotten. Of the rewards, the greatest is the personal satisfaction which comes with the consciousness of having fulfilled an artistic ideal. Such exultation, which is priceless because it cannot be bought, is a part of the instinct of the true artist. It is felt by the player no less than by the workers in the other artistic professions, but with this difference, that the player always has tangible proof of the success of what he is attempting to do in the applause and response of his audience. It is the happy fortune of the actor that the public does not wait until he is dead to decide the value of the work he has performed.

The material reward of the actor is also high. The success of the work he does may be the result of the weeks of drill he has received from others, but nevertheless he gets the pay, revels in the applause, and yet assumes none of the financial risk of the enterprises in which he is concerned. I know of no other profession in which the scale of salaries has so rapidly increased. In the earlier day of the theatre, when no man or woman entered its stage door because he or she considered it the "easiest way," its great artists received no pay at all.

What they got in return was their love for its work and their satisfaction in its accomplishment. An only ordinary actor nowadays earns twenty times as much money compensation as a genius of the past, and he also expects much more consideration. I do not believe equal good fortune extends to the other arts and professions.

Whenever any young person, especially a young woman, shows an inclination to go on the stage, the question of her moral welfare instantly rises. Let the same young woman, with equally good intentions, decide to enter some other professional calling or take up a business career, and the matter of morals is never brought into consideration.

The theatre has its temptations, but so has the studio, or factory, or shop, or any other vocation in which an unprotected woman may be placed. Girls have been known to make missteps even in the home where they are safeguarded on every side. If any young woman has the honest desire to do right and the will to command the respect of others and preserve her own self-respect, I think she is probably as safe in the theatre as anywhere else. Of course she will be subject to temptation, but the influences which will threaten her are more likely to come from without the theatre than from within.

The disadvantage at which she is always

placed is that she becomes at once a more or less public personage and must endure the idle, baseless gossip that meddles in the affairs of all other people similarly placed. I have known thousands of men and women of the theatre whose lives have been beyond suspicion or reproach; the ones who have gone downward are, after all, in a small minority, and the proportion just about corresponds to the relative good and bad in human nature generally.

The trouble is that the moralists who are so constantly worried about the snares in the path of the people of the stage in most cases know little or nothing of the inside of the theatre. The press helps to spread the mistaken notion that the normal life of the actor must be the gay life. The victims of the daily routine of the police courts are always ready to classify themselves as "actresses." Whenever their records are investigated it is discovered, in seven cases out of ten, or even more, that they have no connection with the theatre whatever. They are taken at their word and thus the decent people of an honorable calling are forever being smirched. The conclusion follows, therefore, that dissipation is more prevalent among stage people than in the other professions.

The girl who goes into the theatre with honest intent will have no time for dissipation. The other players with whom she will associate will not tolerate conduct that is unseemly. Outside the theatre she is liable to meet with the lures that are constantly set for any unprotected girl in the life of our great cities, but whether she resists or succumbs to them depends upon herself alone. If fall she will, the descent in the department store or the office building is quite as convenient and swift.

On the other hand, no woman can be a prude in the theatre. She cannot run home to her mother if everything does not go to her liking. She must learn to take a broad and liberal view of its peculiar and unconventional life and of people and things around her, and to bear with fortitude the disappointments which are sure to fall to her lot. She will need courage, stamina, and a reasonable amount of philosophy. If she have the instinct of self-protection and the determination to do right, there is no doubt she will come through her experiences without contamination.

If as much were known of the rough road of the theatre as of the other professions, I do not think so many people would surrender to the craving to try to become actors. At least more would consider the step very seriously before they present themselves at the manager's office or the stage door. Though the mail never ceases to bring its burden of applications, I try to make it a point never to leave a letter unanswered. At such times I do not fail to recall an experience of my own long ago, when my career in the theatre was just beginning in California.

Though still a young lad, I had played small parts in traveling companies up and down the Pacific coast, and followed the hard life of the strolling actor in Virginia City and among the lawless mining-camps of Idaho. But I knew all the time that this experience would not take me far, and a great desire seized me to go back to San Francisco so that I might study the famous stars who came regularly to the old California Theatre, which was then at the height of its prestige.

Soon after I arrived Lawrence Barrett came to the California and I made up my mind to try for a place, however obscure it might be, in his company. I spent a week composing the letter in which I asked him to hear me recite. I poured my whole soul into the story of my ambitions. Then I waited, eagerly at first, finally in utter dejection, for the reply which was never to come.

In the following year I returned to San Francisco and saw John McCullough act Virginius at the same theatre. His emotional power was so tremendous and real that I summoned all the courage there was in me and asked him if he could spare the time to hear me recite. That same afternoon I got his reply, promising to listen to me for half an hour at the theatre on the following Sunday afternoon.

Almost overcome with fear, I presented myself, and mounted the stage while McCullough, with a few friends, sat at a distance back in the dark auditorium. Then, with beating heart, I plunged eloquently into Mrs. Heman's "Bernardo del Carpis," which was one of the favorite school recitations of that day.

> The warrior bowed his crested head
> And tamed his steed of fire,
> And sued the haughty King to free
> His long-imprisoned sire—

When I had finished the great tragedian appeared pleased and said he would like to hear me read something more. His pleasant manner gave me new courage and I summoned "The Vagabond" and "The Stutterer" from my ready *repertoire.*

"And now," asked McCullough, "can't you read me something a little more dramatic?"

I recalled at once the old poem, "The Madman." It surely was dramatic, but the clothes I wore were hardly suitable for a madman's rôle. Asking McCullough to excuse me a moment, I slipped out of my coat. On the floor happened to be some providential straws which I stuck into my thick black hair.

Then my tussle with "The Madman" began. If my very life had been at stake I could not

[39]

have worked myself up to finer frenzies. When I came to the finish of my maniacal exhibition I discovered with dismay that I had torn both sleeves of my shirt to tatters. McCullough and his friends applauded, and then the great actor pleasantly bade me good-by.

The very next morning he sent me a letter offering me a good position in his company. That is why now, night after night, I go down on the stage of the Belasco Theatre after the performance is over, and listen to recitations and readings by people who think the planets in the heavens ordained that they should act. I know the percentage who have ability will be woefully small, but I cannot forget at such times the kindly encouragement and helping hand that John McCullough held out to me.

David Belasco in the Workroom of His Studio in the Belasco Theatre, Before the Fireplace Which Contains Seventy-three Tiles Taken from the Alhambra at Granada, Spain

Mrs. Leslie Carter and Hamilton Revelle

In a scene from "Du Barry" when Mrs. Carter was Mr. Belasco's leading emotional star

Chapter II

THE EVOLUTION OF A PLAY

I

IN a time like the present, when the stage appeals so intimately to the interest of a great majority of all classes of the public, the tendency is natural to regard its art lightly. The observation and experience of those of us who are within the theatre lead to the conclusion that nearly every one is not only a playgoer, but, at one time or another, aspires to write or even tries to write a play.

These aspirants who attempt to express their impressions of life and character in action and the spoken word are, of course, seldom qualified for what is, I believe, the most difficult of all tasks in the domain of the arts. They do not realize that, no matter how valuable or interesting the idea they seek to present may be, it can be accomplished only with a thorough technical knowledge, which is very hard to acquire, of so complicated and treacherous an instrument of artistic expression as the stage. People who have proved failures in the various professions and scientific pursuits turn confidently as a last resort to the much more baffling vocation of playwriting. Propagandists attempt to appropriate the theatre as a convenient means of ventilating their theories, forgetting that however attractive the theories themselves may be, an interesting presentation of them in terms of drama is an entirely different matter.

It is a common impulse of sentimental women to want to write plays, and thousands of them try. So, also, do numerous others as alien to the profession of letters as the business man, the society woman, the housemaid, or even the cook. I sometimes wonder if the true explanation for this very general passion to write for the theatre is not that the really well-made play seems so spontaneous and easy of accomplishment. Since all people talk and act constantly in every-day life, why, they reason, should it be hard to make characters talk and act on the stage?

With such a large part of the population trying to write plays which they expect the other part will applaud, it is no wonder the constant complaint of all dramatic producers, that they cannot find suitable material for their stages, is generally heard with skepticism. It is never impossible for the producer to obtain plays—they pour down upon him in avalanches; but to find in this mass of unsolicited contributions even an occasional manuscript which meets the requirements of what a play ought to be is a quite different thing. In every profession one must catch his hare before he can cook it; the difficulty in the profession of the dramatic producer is that hares worth cooking are so few and far between.

Every manager of established reputation follows his own method of obtaining plays and preparing them for public performance. In this respect the art of the stage differs from all other arts, since, having to meet so many varying conditions and contingencies, it cannot be regulated by hard and fast rules of procedure. To a certain extent, also, a producer cannot restrict himself to a single process in all the plays he himself presents. But there should be, nevertheless, a common denominator which establishes the individuality of his work and determines the artistic value of the results which he accomplishes.

In my own experience I have always found it very difficult to obtain the kind of dramas I have wanted to produce. Compared with this constant search for plays which I have kept up with all my energy for more than thirty years, the actual work of making my productions, complicated and difficult as it is, once the play which is suitable to my purpose has been found, becomes relatively easy, for it does not involve to nearly so great a degree the element of chance.

I have always endeavored to be first in the field with plays that are out of the stage's conventional groove, and that, at the same time, are likely to appeal to the public's constantly changing taste. When I established the theatres in New York which bear my name, manuscripts poured in on me in such numbers that I could not possibly find time to so much as glance over them. It occurred to me that, if I established a play bureau and placed it in charge of competent readers, it would be a courtesy and encouragement to ambitious writers and at the same time might prove of great advantage to me.

I gave my idea a thorough test. At much expense I organized my bureau, at first with one reader, but soon I had to increase the number to three. Before long we were receiving from four thousand to five thousand manuscripts each season. All were carefully read, and, if any seemed especially inviting, they were turned over to me to examine, while the others were sent back to the authors with comments pointing out their defects. But during the whole period that the play bureau was continued, and in spite of the thousands of manuscripts sent to it, I never found even one which I dared to produce.

This disappointment of my expectations is not as remarkable as it may seem. It agrees with the experiences of other managers. The late Charles Frohman once told me that, among all the thousands of unsolicited plays sent to him during more than twenty years, he had never found even one which he could accept. Later I believe this record was broken, for Mr. Frohman, just before his death when the *Lusitania* was torpedoed, accepted "The Hyphen," one of the first of the spy plays that followed the outbreak of the war in Europe, which had dropped in on him out of the nowhere. It failed completely in two weeks.

My play bureau proved to be not only of no advantage to me, but it became a source of endless complaints and frequent lawsuits. It was inevitable that manuscripts which I had never seen should contain plots and incidents somewhat similar to other plays I afterward produced. So after every success in my theatre I found myself being sued by unknown writers. I had no difficulty in contesting these claims when they were actually carried into the courts, but they cost me much time, money, and annoyance. When, finally, a Coney Island barber charged me with stealing the plot of "The Woman" from a play by him, which I had never heard of, I abolished the play bureau in disgust.

Play brokers constantly submit to me dramas which they think suitable to my purposes, or to the needs of my stars. I keep in close touch with foreign authors and with the stages of

Europe, and I obtain the refusal of their original plays or of the American rights. I am generally engaged in writing a play of my own. I also assist by advice a number of young writers who submit ideas or plots which impress me as capable of development into good plays. This process is slow, of course, but as a rule it has brought me excellent results.

It is much easier for a producer to select a play and then cast it effectively than to find a suitable vehicle for a star. I can look with confidence to established native and foreign playwrights for dramas to be acted by special companies, but almost always I have found it necessary to write the plays for my stars, or, if I have happened to find one reasonably suited to the ability of a certain star, I have been obliged either to rewrite it or have it rewritten by the author. In a star's play there must be a perfect adjustment of the principal character to the temperament and ability of its interpreter, or else it is better not to produce it at all.

Almost invariably the exceptionally successful play is not written, but rewritten. However attractive it may seem in the form in which it comes to the producer, it is capable of improvement. This axiom of the theatre, which is as old as the theatre itself, has been verified again and again in my own experience.

A few years ago I had written a play for one

of my stars.   The scenery was already painted and the cast had been partly engaged when, with a new season only six months distant, I found my plans suddenly changed.   In my dilemma I thought over the plays I had read or seen, and happened to remember a piece called "Juanita" which I had come across in a stock theatre in Los Angeles.   It was a story of southern California, and, being a Californian myself, it naturally had appealed strongly to me.   In describing how Frances Starr came under my management I have already made reference to this play.   Its heroine was a young Spanish girl and I saw at once that Miss Starr would play the character well.   But aside from the pretty romance the play contained, it had impressed me as very crude.

I sent for its author, Richard Walton Tully, and together we spent five months revising it. At the end of that time the romance of the story had been expanded, its crudeness had disappeared, and the play had been renamed "The Rose of the Rancho."   But there was still something about it which did not seem to justify me in risking a new and comparatively unknown actress in its leading rôle.   So Mr. Tully and I went at it again.   We changed it not once, but a dozen times.   At last we whipped it into the form I desired.   This laboriously revised and rebuilt play, with Miss Starr in its title rôle, became one of my great successes.

I have followed this same process with every play I have produced, except "The Easiest Way" and "The Secret." Having been successful with two short Oriental plays, "The First Born" and "Madame Butterfly," I was anxious to present a substantial drama of Japanese life. A great many years ago I had written a play dealing with Italian character and containing certain situations which, it seemed to me, might be adapted to a Japanese locale. John Luther Long was the author of the story from which "Madame Butterfly" had been taken, so I invited him to collaborate with me on the new play I had in mind, as he possessed an intimate knowledge of the traits of character of the Japanese. The play we wrote together was "The Darling of the Gods." We did the work with a great deal of facility and were much pleased with it when the first draft was completed; nevertheless, before it finally reached the stage we had taken it apart and entirely rewritten it, not once, but several times.

The exceptional popularity of one of my more recent comedy productions, "The Boomerang," has caused a good deal of favorable comment. Theatregoers who have been impressed by the spontaneity and ease with which it seemed to have been written may be surprised to know that, having submitted it to me in a form which they thought complete,

Winchell Smith and Victor Mapes, its authors, worked on it for nearly two more years, and at my suggestion rewrote it completely three times. Their task grew very irksome and sometimes they became greatly discouraged, but surely the results justified the energy and time which the revisions required.

I have always made it a practice to be not less critical of my own plays. When "The Girl of the Golden West" left my desk, the manuscript was decked out with blue ribbons and I regarded it with the natural pride of an author who had lavished his best efforts upon it. I then put it aside for a time. When I took it up again several weeks later I determined to attack it impersonally. I said to myself:

"I shall pretend that this play was written by 'Smith,' and that some producer has paid me a thousand dollars to adapt it for him. I shall try to forget that I have ever had anything to do with its original script and shall revise it from the point of view of an experienced stage-manager. Moreover, I shall do the work as deliberately as if I had no interest in its immediate production."

So I began rewriting, changing, and adapting. Speeches that merely read well, without advancing the action or elaborating the characters, I cut out altogether. Scenes that were effective, but unnecessary to the story, I ruth-

lessly slaughtered. By the time I had finished, I, as Belasco, had several times broken
'Smith's' heart. But I think I also greatly
improved my own play.

I follow this system with every author who
works for or with me. Every detail of a play
which I intend to produce I analyze and debate,
pro and con, with him. But I try never to
force my own convictions upon a writer. I
ask him to listen to whatever criticisms I may
make, and then, if I succeed in impressing him
that I am right, we have a basis to work on.
The first law of the stage, whether in writing
a play or playing a part, is to convince the
audience of the truth and logic of the work.
Let this supreme quality be absent and the
play, however great may be the care lavished
on its literary execution or production, will be
a failure.

How complete should be the equipment of
the dramatist, and also the producer who
brings his drama into life, is best expressed by
saying that playwriting is the most complex
of all the arts. The dramatist must furnish a
complete foundation for every detail of the
work which falls upon the producer or stage
director. The play once in hand, the producer
must possess an artist's sense of colors. He
must be a close student of nature. He must
be familiar with geography and the manners
and customs of peoples. He should be a dan-

David Belasco at Work on the Preliminaries of a Play in the
Workroom of His Studio

Photograph taken just before the production of "The Easiest Way"

David Belasco with the Heads of His Artistic and Mechanical Departments

They are building a miniature stage-setting of the play, "Marie-Odile." Every stage-setting used at the Belasco Theatre is built from an exact miniature model which is fully equipped, even to the lighting cer—at least rhythm must be a part of his soul, for action is the poetry of motion. He should be careful to inform himself on any special subject that may enter the work he is preparing for the stage. When the play fails in its intent, he, not the author or the actors, is usually to blame. The impression which the completed work is destined to make rests with him.

In preparing the production of "The Return of Peter Grimm," I studied with diligence such standard books on psychic phenomena as Prof. James H. Hyslop's *Psychical Research and The Resurrection* and Fremont Rider's *Are the Dead Alive?* and I had several long talks with Professor James. I did not undertake "The Case of Becky," which dealt with the phenomenon of dual personality, until I was thoroughly familiar with Prof. Morton Price's work, *The Dissociation of a Personality*, and I had for a time, as my guest, Professor Allen, of Philadelphia, who was also present three days at the final rehearsals. When art intrudes upon the domain of science it should have authority for everything it appropriates.

I recall that when I produced "Men and Women" twenty years ago, I obtained the atmosphere of the Directors' Meeting scene which it contained by going to a real directors' meeting in a Wall Street bank, where I sat in a corner and watched the proceedings. To get the right feeling for "The Man Inside" I engaged "Chuck" Connors, a Bowery denizen now dead, to take me on a slumming tour among Chinese opium-joints, and I even went down near the Tombs Prison at 2 A.M. to listen to sounds in the vicinity, such as the clocks striking the hours.

Both as playwright and producer I am a realist, but I do not believe in harrowing audiences unnecessarily. It was very hard to avoid one distressing scene in my own play, "The Return of Peter Grimm," but I overcame the defect after experimenting with it several weeks. The play dealt with the persistent survival of personality, or, as some people would have it, with a ghost. For the dénouement of the story it was necessary that the returned spirit of old Peter should become visible to one of the characters. I first invented a séance scene with a woman medium, but in rehearsals it impressed me as ridiculous. Then, after various experiments, none of which quite satisfied me, I hit upon the idea of writing into the play the character of a little child and having him, in his dying delirium, see old Peter in his spirit presence. I was aware that the scene of the child's death would be painful to the audience if I did not soften it, so I introduced into the opening act the effect of a circus passing the house with bands playing and clowns singing, to the delight of the child as he stood at the window. Then, when the death scene was reached at the end of the play, I reproduced all these circus sounds, but softly and from far away, as if they were passing through the little child's disordered mind, and he died smiling and happy. So the effect upon the audience, while deeply pathetic, was neither harsh nor cruel.

II

Let us now assume that a play has been brought into acceptable form in its manuscript and I have made up my mind to produce it. My first step in the practical work of production is to study out the scenes, which must be constructed as carefully as the play itself, for a skilfully devised scene is always of vital assistance to an episode. In this preliminary work I seldom follow the stage directions on the printed page, either of my own plays or those of other dramatists. I prefer to plan the scenes myself with reference to stage values.

I consider where a window or door, a balcony or a fireplace, will be most effective. The feeling of the scene is always a great factor in determining its arrangement, for symbolism to a certain extent enters the production of every play. For instance, sunlit scenes imply happiness, moonlit scenes give a suggestion of romance, while tragedy or sorrow should be played in gloom. It is never advisable to stage comedy scenes, which depend for their interest upon the wittiness of the dialogue, in exterior settings, for the surroundings suggest too great an expanse; if acted in an interior setting the lines become immeasurably more effective.

Such details as these must be carefully thought out, and as I become more familiar with the lines and episodes the scenes gradually form themselves. Then I make a rough sketch, taking into account the necessary arrangement of furniture or other properties and considering how the characters can be maneuvered to best advantage.

When I have settled these matters approximately, I send for my scenic artist. With him seated in front, I take the empty stage and, as far as possible, try to act the whole play, making every entrance and exit and indicating my ideas of the groupings of the characters and their surroundings. This process, which would probably seem farcical to a casual onlooker, will consume perhaps four or five evenings, for not one detail can be left to chance or put aside until I am satisfied that it cannot be improved.

During this process one must treat the play as a human being; it must laugh at certain points, at others it must be sad; lovers must come together in certain lights; and all its changing moods must be blended harmoniously. For the completed play is impressive and fulfils its purpose only to the extent that it carries an audience back to its own experiences. If my productions have had an appealing quality, it is because I have kept this important fact constantly in mind and have tried, while concealing the mechanism of my scenes, to tug at the hearts of my audiences.

Having explained in detail my ideas and turned over a manuscript to him, the scenic artist proceeds to make a drawing of the scenes, following my crude sketches, and thus we reach a definite starting-point. In due course of time—it may be a week or a month—the scenic artist will have constructed the actual scene models which are set up in the perfectly equipped miniature theatre of my studio. But changes are always suggesting themselves, and often these models, which are about four feet long, have to be taken apart and reconstructed several times.

It is time now to begin to consider what to me is the all-important factor in a dramatic production—the lighting of the scenes. With my electrician I again go over the play in detail, very much according to the method I have previously followed with my scenic artist. When he has thoroughly grasped my ideas and become quite familiar with the play itself, we begin our experiments, using the miniature theatre and evolving our colors by transmitting white light through gelatin or silk of various hues. Night after night we experiment together to obtain color or atmospheric effects, aiming always to make them aid the interpretation of the scenes.

Lights are to drama what music is to the lyrics of a song. No other factor that enters into the production of a play is so effective in conveying its moods and feeling. They are as essential to every work of dramatic art as blood is to life. The greatest part of my success in the theatre I attribute to my feeling for colors, translated into effects of light. Sometimes these effects have been imitated by other producers with considerable success, but I do not fear such encroachments. It may be possible for others to copy my colors, but no one can get my feeling for them.

The lighting effects on my stages have been secured only after years of experiment and at an expense which many other producers would consider ridiculous. Sometimes I have spent five thousand dollars attempting to reproduce the delicate hues of a sunset and then have thrown the scene away altogether. I recall that when I produced "The Girl of the Golden West," I experimented three months to secure exactly the soft, changing colors of a Californian sunset over the Sierra Nevadas, and then turned to another method. It was a good sunset, but it was not Californian. Afterward I sold it to the producers of "Salomy Jane," and it proved very effective and perfectly adjusted to the needs of that play.

These experiments have always been the most interesting part of my work as a producer, although they have also been the most perplexing and sometimes the most baffling. It is no easy matter, for instance, to indicate the difference between the moon and stars of a Japanese night and the fanciful moon and stars of fairyland. But there is, nevertheless, a difference which an audience must be made to feel, without detecting the mechanism, just as one is conscious of heat, yet does not see it, on entering a warm room.

The problem of lighting was especially difficult in my production of "The Return of Peter Grimm," since in that play it was necessary to indicate the contrast between life and death. Doing away with footlights helped me considerably, but it took five months of experiments to accomplish the results I sought. I invented special reflectors to produce the ashen hue of death, but something always seemed lacking. I kept David Warfield in New York all summer, standing alone on the stage for hours at a stretch, while I threw various lights upon him. Then it occurred to me that the trouble lay in the kind of clothes he wore. I sent for fifty bolts of cloth and wrapped him in the different fabrics and colors, until I found one which made him look mysterious and far away. Even then his appearance was not quite right. When other characters came on the stage things went wrong. Finally I tried the expedient of casting a cold gray light upon his features from above, while, at the same time, I illuminated the faces of the other characters in the play with a faint rosy glow. It was necessary to have many of these lights of differing quality which, one after the other, "picked up" the people as they moved from place to place on the stage. The effect was exactly what I desired, and it proved to be one of the most important factors in the success of the play.

In my production of "The Darling of the Gods" in 1902 it was comparatively easy to indicate by lights the tragic feeling of the scene in which the band of Samurai commit suicide by hari-kari. I set the stage in the picture of a gaunt bamboo forest, behind which was a great blood-red setting sun to symbolize ebbing life. In the shadows Kara's followers could be faintly seen and the audience could hear the clatter of their lacquered armor as they went to their self-inflicted deaths.

But when it came to the scene of the River of Souls, in which the dead were to swim to the lower depths, or purgatory, in preparation to entering the celestial hereafter, a most troublesome problem arose. I had built the translucent scene of the river at a cost of $6,500 and had devised a kind of harness in which fifteen girls were suspended to represent the passage of the souls. When I tested the scene with manikins in my miniature theatre, it invariably worked perfectly; but when I tried it on the regular stage something was sure to go wrong. Some of the girls swam well, while others swam badly, and almost always one or two got tangled in their harness. Such accidents in a performance before an audience would have caused laughter, which would have been fatal to a production that had cost $80,000.

For two days and two nights, barring short recesses, we worked over that stubborn scene, and at last I decided to give it up. Blanche Bates, who was to play the character of the heroine, Yo-San, was almost in despair. George Arliss lay asleep on a lounge at the side of the stage, and every one else was vexed, discouraged, and completely fagged out. The opening performance had already been twice postponed, but reluctantly I made up my mind to put it off again.

I ordered the scene "struck," and my carpenters hoisted all the opaque setting which had been made at great cost, leaving a single gauze curtain suspended in irregular folds at the front of the stage. Just at this moment one of the workmen happened to pass between the curtain and a light at the back. Seen through the folds of the curtain his movements were almost ghostly. I saw at once that the effect for which I had been striving had come to me ready-made. Each of the fifteen girls was told to count ten and then cross the stage, using her arms to suggest a kind of swimming motion. The effect was remarkable, for the number of figures seemed increased a thousand-fold. Having already thrown away $6,500, I built the scene in a day for $90 and it is being imitated yet.

In "Du Barry" one of the problems which arose was how to change from a brilliantly lighted scene to a dark scene without abruptly turning out the lights, and also how to invent an excuse for the ensuing darkness. I thought of midnight bathing and other pastimes of the court of Louis XV, but I could not put them on the stage. While looking over some books on the customs of the period, I ran across descriptions of the lighted balls which were tossed about by the courtiers and ladies in court games. Thus I not only found the excuse I needed for turning out my stage lights, but the brilliantly illuminated balls did away with the abruptness of the change, while the novelty of it appealed strongly to the audience at a point in the play where a surprise was needed to stimulate its interest.

THE EVOLUTION OF A PLAY

The scene models having been approved and the very important matter of the lighting being well under way, it is time now to begin the building of the actual scenes. I turn my carpenters over to my scenic artist, who furnishes to them the plans. They then construct the scenery in my own shops, for I never have such work done by contract. I will allow nothing to be built out of canvas stretched on frames. Everything must be real. I have seen plays in which thrones creaked on which monarchs sat, and palace walls flapped when persons touched them. Nothing so destructive to illusion or so ludicrous can happen on my stage.

Meanwhile, if the play has a musical accompaniment, I read it to the composer I have engaged, indicating its moods and feeling. He must interpret every scene and speech as if he were writing the score for a song. I always aim to avoid fitting old or familiar music to a new play.

I generally prefer to leave the costuming until after the first week of rehearsals, when I am reasonably sure of my actors, unless it happens to be a costume play which I am producing. If it demands other than modern clothes, I write a full description for the characters, deciding whether their hair shall be smooth or shaggy and whether they shall or shall not wear beards, and then call a costume-designer into consultation. All this is very necessary in a costume play, in order to preserve the color harmonies of my scenes. If, on the other hand, it be a modern play that I am producing, I send my actors, when the proper time comes, to the various shops to be fitted for their clothing.

I try not to dictate too much in the matter of dresses for my actresses, except to preserve the color harmonies, but I insist that they must take heed of the temperament of the characters they are to represent and the stations in life to which ·the characters belong. As for the male characters, if one would be likely to purchase his clothes of a fashionable tailor, I send the actor to just such a shop; if another would be likely to wear cheap, ready-made stuff, he must seek it in that kind of a place. Clothes, to be sure, do not make the man, but generally they are a safe index to his character and temperament.

While all these various details of the production are moving along, except the costuming, to which I have referred incidentally, I am hunting everywhere for my cast. In fact, I have been on the lookout for actors and actresses suitable to the various characters from the moment I made up my mind to accept the play. Applicants for parts come to my office in swarms, but generally they are members of the profession who are too familiarly known to the public, since I prefer, as far as possible, to develop my own actors. I ransack the varieties and the cheap stock companies, and I both go to see the people and have them come to see me. If I happen to be producing a play for a star, the organization of the company is somewhat simplified, but in any event I always choose my players with the greatest care. In making my selections I would much prefer to have an actor resemble the character he is to represent than have him depend upon disguise and the assumption of manners, for my motto as a producer has been to keep as close to nature as possible.

By the time I am ready to make my contracts, my conception of every character is complete. Should the character be English or French or Italian, I try to engage actors of those nationalities to impersonate them. When I was preparing the production of "The Music Master," I searched for some of my people in the theatres of the lower East Side of New York; in "The Darling of the Gods" I employed Japanese in some instances; in "Marie-Odile" my Uhlans were real Germans.

It is necessary, also, to be quite as careful in selecting supers as in engaging people for speaking rôles. Sometimes I have gathered together one hundred and fifty super candidates at one sitting, and from this number have chosen barely half a dozen. I study their features closely, with a view to their fitness, and I watch their manner and movements.

In the case of players of speaking rôles the quality of the voice is a strong persuading factor in my calculations. If I happen to have selected an actor with a deep voice for a certain part, I try to put him opposite an actress who has a highly pitched voice, for when the talk floats across the footlights it must blend as in a song. In casting a play for a star, I am also careful to avoid temperamental people, for it must be the star who has the monopoly of temperamental qualities. Such small details as these are not ordinarily noticed by audiences; nevertheless, they are unconsciously felt, and consequently they become of utmost importance in every artistic production of a drama.

III

I have been dealing, up to this point, with what, to a theatre audience, are the impersonal factors in the evolution of a play on my stage. Until my company is fully organized its members, of course, remain scattered. In due course of time — I usually allot about six weeks to rehearsals of a play which does not offer unusual difficulties—notices are sent out for the people to assemble. When they arrive at the theatre I always make it a practice to be on hand to receive them. I want them to feel from the outset an intimate relationship to me and to one another. Some have already played together in the same companies; some know one another only by reputations, and some are strangers. I introduce them to one another and treat them as guests in my drawing-room, rather than as employees on my stage. After a few moments spent in general conversation I then invite them to accompany me to the reading-room, where they find a long, well-lighted table surrounded by comfortable chairs.

When we are all seated—I at the head of the table with the scene models beside me—I invariably give a few preliminary instructions. First of all I caution the members of the company not to discuss the play outside my theatre. I impress upon them that the ultimate result of our efforts will depend upon the spirit of co-operation which each brings to it and that the success of the whole is more important to me than any of its parts. I urge that they must not judge the value of their characters by the number of lines allotted to them to speak, but rather by the artistry which the characters permit. Above all, I ask them not to be selfish, but to assist one another because, after all, they are only the component parts of a single picture.

My sermon preached and reiterated, I then read the play from beginning to end, without interruptions or comments. This ceremony finished, the individual parts are distributed by the prompter.

Luncheon is then served in the reading-room, and presently we return to the play, this time with the actors reading their own parts. We pause frequently for discussions, and I am now on the alert to detect the inevitable errors by the typist. When words or phrases do not seem to be understood, we try to decide them at once. Whenever the play involves the frequent use of French or German words, I aim to have teachers of those languages present at the reading, and their decisions become our court of last appeal. Meanwhile I counsel the people to give close heed to the characteristic inflections of the rôles they are to perform. For instance, I would not permit an Englishman to say "can't or sha'n't," nor would I allow an American character to say "caunt" or "shaunt." In life people speak variously. Therefore it is advisable, in the rehearsal of a play, not to restrict actors to conventional pronunciations. Within the limits of good usage, I prefer them to take their choice.

Talk about stage-fright! The suffering of actors at a first public performance is nothing compared to what they undergo when, with no one but myself present, they first read their parts from the manuscript. Each character is closely analyzed as we proceed. Invariably our discussions bring out more of the psychology of the rôles than the author ever dreamed his play contained. When the reading is finished we indulge in a little general conversation—the pleasant social relationship of the members of a theatrical company is always important—and then the rehearsal is adjourned until the following morning.

Daily, at the same hour, ten-thirty o'clock, we assemble in the reading-room. The actors have not yet memorized their parts, but are reading from the manuscript. Each one is acquiring a better conception of his own rôle and noticing the gradual growth of the other characters. Meanwhile I study the individual actors, noting where values and deficiencies lie. I observe when they cannot sustain scenes or speeches—when they are not good listeners—and make up my mind what I am going to do when I get them on my stage.

During this week of preliminary readings I rarely fail to detect imperfections which have previously escaped my notice, in the play itself. I follow the construction in an effort to find weak spots. There may be no "carrying over" interest between episodes or scenes, and these must be corrected. I may say in this connection that I have rarely been opposed by my authors when changes in their manuscripts have been found necessary; they have generally been willing to yield to my judgment. So, whether it may be my own or another's play, I rewrite, transpose, change, and cut, until, at the end of a week, the manuscripts are so interlined that it is almost impossible to read them. In more than the average case the manuscripts must be retyped —plays, I repeat, are built, not written— and at this point we are ready for our first real rehearsal.

When I am satisfied that the members of the company have in their minds a clear conception of the play and its characters—up to this point they have been only reading and listening, not acting—I make it a rule to turn them over to my stage director, who supervises them during the first rehearsal on the stage. He, in the mean time, has been studying the play and listening to the readings, and knows, roughly at least, what I am aiming to accomplish. I have always found it better to keep out of sight during the first experiments in the real acting, for when I am present the actors stand still and depend upon me for directions.

I always caution the stage director to let them give him everything, that he must give them nothing. In this way they rely upon their own initiative and, so to speak, squeeze themselves dry. Their invention seems to grow when they know they can do as they please. With this confidence gained, I take control of the play again and we go at it in earnest.

Now the period of hardest work has been reached. I have kept my people on the stage twenty hours at a stretch, making some of them read a single line perhaps fifty times, experimenting with little subtleties of intonation or gesture, and going over bits of business again and again. Infinite patience is needed to make others understand the soul of a character as the author or producer conceives it, and such patience, coupled with the knack of communicating his own ideas, must be possessed by every successful producer.

I have never resorted to bullying in order to make my actors do as I wish; I have always found that the best results can be gained by appealing subtly to their imagination. I can convey more to them by a look or a gesture than by a long harangue or a scolding.

Peculiarities in the actors are also disclosed by these experiments. Some may be able to speak their lines more effectively while seated than while standing; some play better on the right side of the stage than on the left, or *vice versa;* one arrives at his best results deliberately, another by nervous energy; I have even known actors whose work varied according to whether they directly faced the audience or presented their profiles to it. Experience has taught me not to direct my players arbitrarily, but to be guided by what they can best do. Their peculiarities are the results of temperament and personality, which the intelligent stage director should always attempt to preserve. I try to correct mannerisms when they are bad, for bad mannerisms are as destructive to good acting as weeds to a garden; but when mannerisms are indexes of personality they have a distinct value.

One of the most frequent errors of dramatic criticism is to condemn the peculiarities of manner, gesture, and elocution which are really the distinguishing signs of histrionic ability. It is upon these personal oddities that the imitators and caricaturists of important players invariably seize. To caricature the late Henry Irving it was necessary only to exaggerate the hollow intonation of his delivery. In Joseph Jefferson's case it was his lisp and quavering utterance which were emphasized. Ellen Terry's bouncing freedom of movement made her acting easy to copy. The liquid speech and the peculiar poise of the head render it easy for such clever impersonators as Cecilia Loftus and Elsie Janis to suggest the manner of Ethel Barrymore, while other traits, inseparable from their personalities, make Maude Adams, Frances

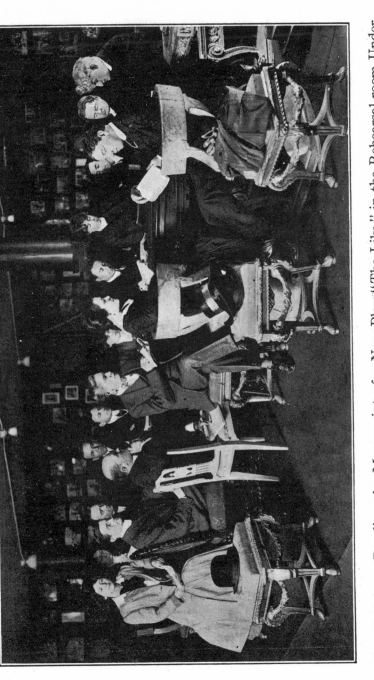

David Belasco Reading the Manuscript of a New Play, "The Lily," in the Rehearsal-room Under the Auditorium of the Belasco Theatre

He always does this before the beginning of rehearsals of a play, following out the old practice of Augustin Daly

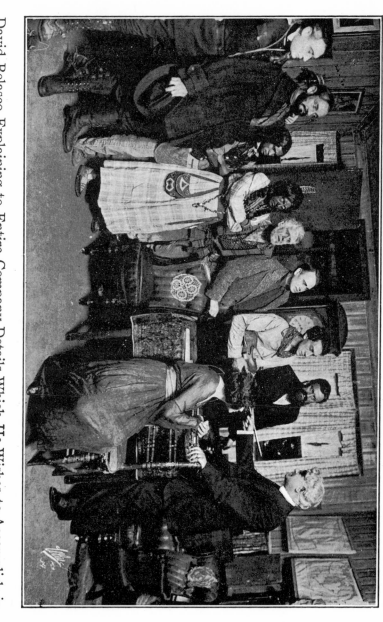

David Belasco Explaining to Entire Company Details Which He Wishes to Accomplish in
One of the Acts of "Tiger Rose".

Taken during a rehearsal at the Belasco Theatre

Starr, and especially Mrs. Fiske shining marks for their humorous copyists.

In other years it was always possible to imitate E. J. Henley by merely intensifying the pauses which recurred constantly in his delivery of the lines of a play. This propensity in his acting was usually referred to deprecatingly as a mannerism, but actually it was one of his most powerful means of expression. Few actors use the pause naturally, and many, in attempting to cultivate it, end by becoming tedious. But when the dramatic pause is uncultivated, it becomes a God-given ability. The actor who employs it spontaneously is not conscious that he is using it. I have often thought, in the case of David Warfield, that the hesitations which punctuate the utterance of his speeches are the true secret of his power and eloquence.

All these idiosyncrasies in my actors I try to preserve, when they are not so pronounced that they seem to be affectations. I direct them so that such personal peculiarities will be put to effective uses. This is one of the reasons why I always work with the company before me. Of late there has sprung up a practice of organizing several companies—in some instances half a dozen—and sending them on tour in plays which happen to have met with unusual popularity in New York. There is a great commercial advantage in such a policy, for it permits the profits of a successful play to be quickly gathered and it simplifies the work of the producer, because invariably the secondary companies attempt no more than to imitate the methods of the original organization. For this reason bad art must inevitably result. Therefore I am opposed to it. I have never directed a second company; if I did, I fear I would change all the business of the play, and possibly make alterations in the play itself. I would discover immediately that what one set of players could do most effectively in a certain manner, another set would have to do in a wholly different way, dependent upon the temperament, personality, and technical equipment of each. When actors attempt only to imitate a model, they become automatons and the artistic finish of both the play and its performance is consequently sacrificed.

So we go over the speeches time after time, generally spending a week or ten days on each act. During this period I have insisted that my actors avoid trying to memorize their rôles until their conception of them is fully formed and they are actually molded into the characters. Otherwise, with every word glibly at their tongues' ends, they will presently begin to talk like parrots. Furthermore, they are always unconsciously studying and memorizing while rehearsing.

Again come the changes—the inevitable changes—in the play. Ways of improving it constantly suggest themselves. If it seems too heavy at a certain point, it must be lightened; if too tearful, laughter must be brought into it. Not a dozen, but a hundred, little touches are sometimes possible. If an excessively talkative scene threatens to tire an audience because of the babel of voices, the effect may be relieved by leaving the stage vacant momentarily in the scene which follows. Paradoxical as it may seem, nothing at times helps a play so much as a momentarily empty stage.

A drama implies a story told in action, but I believe in permitting characters to remain in repose if the conditions under which the story is related demand repose. The natural exposition of the plot of one of my productions, "The Concert," required, in the first act, that the wife of the philandering music-teacher and the husband of his infatuated pupil remain seated and in conversation for forty minutes. During the early rehearsals I was considerably disturbed because I feared that these two characters, with nothing to do but talk, might not be able to hold the interest of the audience. Yet the scene itself was restful, and the inaction seemed perfectly natural. I hesitated three days while I tried to introduce speeches to create "business," but it never quite suited me. The "business" I improvised seemed always to interrupt the drift of the story. At last I took desperate chances and gave instructions to my two players to sit still. On the opening night, still uncertain of the wisdom of my plan, I carefully watched the effect of that scene on the audience. Not for an instant did the long-drawn-out conversation lose its grip upon the attention. The reason was that it was the natural thing for the characters to do. When critics complain that a play "lacks action" it is because there is something other than action which is fundamentally wrong with the play itself. No experience in the world can teach an actor or producer to follow absolute naturalness—the instinct must be born in him.

I change not only details in the play during these rehearsals, but also in the lighting of the stage, for the reason that the spell produced by light is an incalculable aid to the art of the actor. Light has a psychological effect which perhaps he is not able to understand or explain, but he feels it instantly and responds to it, and then the audience just as quickly responds to him. I have sometimes doubled the persuasiveness of a speech, not by changing a word written by the author, or an intonation or gesture by the actor, but by increasing the value of the light in which the character stands. The secret is that it is much easier to appeal to the hearts of audiences through their senses than through their intellects. People go to the play to have their emotions stirred. When they respond they become a part of the play itself. We on the stage instantly feel this subtle influence, so they really give us more than we give them.

The rehearsals up to this time have been held first on an empty stage and then, as the actors have gradually gained in proficiency, with substitute scenery. Each act has been attacked singly, without proceeding to the next until the one in hand runs perfectly smoothly. Then comes the day when, still using the substitute scenery, all the acts are put together for the first time. At this first consecutive rehearsal of the entire play I am very easy with my people, as it seems to require all their vitality and strength. But they grow into it quickly, for by this time I have drilled the company until the words of their parts have become like the ones they learned to lisp in childhood. If I have discovered words which they cannot pronounce well, I have changed them; if, under stress of emotion, there are other words which they are likely to slur, I find easier equivalents.

During all the time that rehearsals have been in progress—and perhaps for many weeks or even months before the first reading—other preparations for the production have been going on. Carpenters have been building the scenery in my shop, artists have been painting it at their studios, electricians have been making the paraphernalia for the lighting effects, property men have been manufacturing or buying the various objects needed in their department, and costumers and wig-makers have been at work. All these adjuncts to the play have been timed to be ready when they are needed. At last comes the order to put them together. Then for three or four days my stage resembles a house in process of being furnished. Confusion reigns supreme with carpenters putting on door-knobs, decorators hanging draperies, workmen laying carpets and rugs, and furniture men taking measurements.

Everything has been selected by me in advance. My explorations in search of stage equipment are really the most interesting parts of my work. I attend auction sales and haunt antique-shops, hunting for the things I want. I rummage in stores in the richest as well as in the poorest sections of New York. Many of the properties must be especially made, and it has even happened that I have been compelled to send agents abroad to find exactly the things I need. For instance, I sent an agent to Bath, England, to buy all the principal properties for "Sweet Kitty Bellairs." It was necessary, also, to send to Paris to obtain many of the objects which fitted into the period of "Du Barry." I purchased the old Dutch furniture I used in "The Return of Peter Grimm" fully two years before I had put the finishing touches on the writing of that play, and most of the Oriental paraphernalia of "The Darling of the Gods" I imported direct from Japan.

When I produced "The Easiest Way" I found myself in a dilemma. I planned one of its scenes to be an exact counterpart of a little hall bedroom in a cheap theatrical boarding-house in New York. We tried to build the scene in my shops, but, somehow, we could not make it look shabby enough. So I went to the meanest theatrical lodging-house I could find in the Tenderloin district and bought the entire interior of one of its most dilapidated rooms—patched furniture, threadbare carpet, tarnished and broken gas fixtures, tumble-down cupboards, dingy doors and window-casings, and even the faded paper on the walls. The landlady regarded me with amazement when I offered to replace them with new furnishings.

While the scenery and properties are being put together I lurk around with my note-book in hand, studying the stage, watching for defects in color harmonies, and endeavoring to make every scene conform to the characteristics of the people who are supposed to inhabit them. However great the precaution

I may have observed, I generally decide to make many more changes. Then, when the stage is furnished to my satisfaction, I bring my company up from the reading-room and introduce them to the scenes and surroundings in which they are to live in the play.

IV

There is a vast difference between rehearsing a company on an empty stage and in the fully equipped settings of a play. The change involves retracing many steps which have already been taken, and undoing many things which seemingly have been done well; but I have been unable to discover a way to avoid it. Now we have the actual width and depth of the stage to guide us and we are able to time with mathematical exactness entrances and exits and the movements of the actors from one place to another. When the characters are put into the permanent scenes, the stage director must also consider them from a somewhat different point of view. The players must be adapted to the scene, not the scene to the players, for the effort should always be to lose the identity of the scene and intensify the identity of the characters. I have always been a strong advocate of stage settings which stimulate the imagination of my audiences and at the same time adorn my plays, but first, last, and always I try not to attract the eye when attention should be fixed upon the dialogue.

However carefully I have rehearsed my company, I still find opportunities for beneficial changes. Necessity arises for shifting the positions of the actors. The various properties, each in its appointed place, help to suggest new "business." Details which first seemed very effective to me suddenly lose their value. Since these alterations must inevitably occur, it is very unfair to actors to delay until the final rehearsal before putting them into the scenes in which the public is to see them and in which they are to be judged.

At last, when every little imperfection in the interpretations of the characters has been detected and perfected, I set apart one performance at which I try not to consider the acting, but the play itself. I am on the lookout for repetitions in the dialogue that may have escaped me, unduly emphatic speeches and climaxes that have not been consistently approached. I keep a stenographer beside me taking down notes and suggestions, for I try not to interrupt the performance or interfere with the inspiration of the players. These final changes made, the company is bidden to become letter-perfect in their rôles as they are now developed. This task of unlearning and learning again is one of the hardest that an actor is called upon to perform. It needs a trained mind to do it quickly and successfully.

I make it a practice to allot one entire day for my people to attend to the details of their costumes. Innumerable little purchases and fixings must be made, especially by the women. I utilize this time making the final adjustment of my lights, for I have now decided upon the exact effects I require. It may take hours or, perhaps, a whole day and a night, in a darkened theatre, for the timing of lights is quite as important as the timing of the movements of the players. For instance, the transition from afternoon to sunset must create a perfect illusion, or else, in its abruptness, it will become ridiculous. The perfect lighting of a stage can be accomplished only when the electricians become as familiar with the play as the actors themselves. I may say that I fully appreciate how great is the assistance my productions have gained from these small-paid men. They do not work mechanically, but with their hearts and souls, for, once having comprehended the spirit of the play, they are as dexterous with the appliances for regulating the lights as musicians with their instruments.

In arranging my final lighting effects I give special heed to the complexions and make-ups of my people. I especially try to protect the appearance of the women. Every feature of a woman's face—nose, eyes, cheek-bones, mouth, profile—helps to determine the intensity and color of the light that should be thrown upon it. Always I am an enemy of white lights, for their effect is to make the skin appear pasty. That is why the poor vaudeville girl always has an ordeal to pass through when she comes out on the stage to perform her little specialty.

At about this time, if all the costumes are ready, I hold what I call my "dress parade." I have my actors dress exactly as they are to be seen in the play, with every detail of clothing—shoes, gloves, neckties, wigs, beards, and cosmetics complete—and march them back and forth across the stage. It frequently happens that changes will be advisable in the appearance of some of them, and the time to decide such matters is now. I supply every detail of the wardrobe which actors wear on my stage, whether I am producing a costume drama or a modern comedy. In every respect the production and all that pertains to it must be in perfect harmony. I take pains to caution the players to "make up" with reference to the predominating tone of the lighting of the stage. In my own theatres the dressing-rooms are equipped with rows of electric bulbs of every hue, so that the actors may gauge the exact effect of the pigments which they put on their faces. But when, occasionally,

I have produced plays in other houses than my own, this important precaution has not been possible, and sometimes it has led to grave defects in the appearance of some of the characters.

When I produced "The Heart of Wetona" I gave careful instructions to William Court-leigh how I wanted him to disguise himself as the Comanche Indian Chief, Quanna; but invariably, when he came out before the foot-lights, his face presented a different effect than I had intended. I was mystified for a time, but finally I asked him what was the color of the lights in his dressing-room. He replied that they were white. That solved the mystery immediately, for under white lights he had been trying to contrive an effect which the audience was to see in a scene that was amber in the tone of its illumination. I thereupon gave orders to have amber lights placed around his dressing-mirror, and from that time he found no further difficulty in making Quanna look like a real Indian chief.

The dress parade over, and the time for the dress rehearsals being at hand, I give my attention to a curtain rehearsal. One who is not familiar with the little touches, apart from the play itself, which aid the general effect of a dramatic production may not realize how important it is to have the curtain work in harmony with the feeling of the scene upon which it rises and falls. I have sometimes experimented with a curtain fifty times, raising or lowering it rapidly, slowly, or at medium speed. The curtain men must be taught to feel the climaxes as keenly as the actors and to work in unison with them. This is a good time, also, if the play have a musical accompaniment, to rehearse the score with my orchestra-leader and musicians, and weld them into parts of the completed whole.

We are ready for the final dress rehearsals now. The production, which has been developing day by day for six weeks or more, has become as complete and its performance is as spontaneous as if it were being given before a crowded audience.

The stage is ordered cleared, the actors are sent to their dressing-rooms to get themselves ready, and I take my place, with my scenic artists and others attached to my staff, in the front of the empty theatre. The people are likely to be more nervous than on a real opening night, for they are conscious that they are to be subjected to concentrated criticism from which there is no appeal. In a crowded theatre they are sure of pleasing at least a part of the audience; it is a different affair when they are trying to meet the approval of only one person. The introductory music, if there be music, is played, up goes the curtain, and the performance begins.

I try not to interrupt if it can possibly be avoided, preferring to reserve my criticisms until the end. But if indefensible mistakes occur—if, for instance, a character on leaving a drawing-room forgets his hat or stick or gloves—I am cruel enough in my comments to make sure that the blunder will never occur again. It is too late now for praising, coaxing, or cajoling. I go on the principle that the good things will take care of themselves, but that not a single flaw must be left undetected. The dress rehearsal ended, I commend the company when I can, reprove them when I must, and generally discuss tempo, deportment, and elocution—everything, in fact, that suggests itself to me. Then the curtain is lowered, the scene is "struck," and we go over the play again and again until, so far as I can judge, nothing more remains to be done.

I have never been in favor of following the French system of holding public rehearsals, although the practice is gradually gaining vogue in this country. But at the final dress rehearsal I find it advantageous to invite a dozen or more people. Their presence not only helps my actors, but also assists me. I watch the faces of these guests much more closely than I watch the performance, for their changing expressions enable me to gauge the effect upon them of each little episode or speech, and in this way I sometimes obtain ideas which have not occurred to me before. I do not place much reliance in the compliments they may offer—I depend, rather, on my own intuition of the effect which the play and the actors have produced upon their minds and emotions.

At last comes the day toward which for weeks we have all been looking forward with mingled happiness and misgivings. Every detail of the production, so far as careful forethought and painstaking preparation can anticipate, is complete. We are now ready to give our work its public test. Of late years dramatic producers, no matter how great their confidence in their methods or their certainty of success, rarely risk a first performance of their plays before a New York audience. There are several reasons which dictate this wise precaution. It is so easy to be misled by the kindly enthusiasm of a metropolitan first-night crowd. Such assemblages invariably contain, in large numbers, friends of the author, actors, or management. Various motives will enter to influence the verdict they may pass upon the play and its performance. I do not mean to imply that I distrust the opinion or taste of general audiences in New York on matters pertaining to dramatic art; on the contrary, I believe their views to be more catholic and substantial than any other audience in the world. But in the case of

New York's typical first-night assemblage, personal interests are sure to enter, and it is our business now to court candid judgment that is unbiased either pro or con.

There is an even more important consideration that dictates a preliminary tour for a play before it settles down for the metropolitan run which means so much for its subsequent fate elsewhere. It is an axiom of the profession of the theatre, which has been proved by experience times without number, that only by performing it publicly can all the imperfections of a play be detected. Only by this practical test, also, is the actor able to judge his own work definitely and become conscious of its shortcomings. A score of professional play-judges, whether they be experienced producers or experienced critics, may unanimously vote that a play is perfect, and still it may fall flat when acted before a paid audience. Or, on the other hand, an assemblage of the most liberal-minded producers and critics in the world may unanimously decide that the doom of a play is sealed, and it will be received by audiences with acclaim.

It is this uncertainty which has made the profession of the dramatic author and the dramatic producer through all the centuries of the English-speaking theatre so interesting and at the same time so precarious. They are destined always to match their best effort against the changing whim and taste of an inscrutable and arbitrary public, and they can never be sure of its outcome until that effort is judged in the forum of public opinion. The workers in other branches of the fine arts, in a measure, escape this implacable test. The poet, the painter, or the sculptor, if his effort be worthy, may wait for the judgment that finds merit in what he has done. But the fate of a work of dramatic art is decided abruptly, once and for all.

So we start out. I always aim to arrange for my companies a preliminary tour of from two to four weeks, and during that period the play is subjected to constant revision. The speeches which, in rehearsals, I thought would produce a thrill may be received in silence. The situation which seemed so sure to compel tears may provoke smiles. In a dozen ways, perhaps, effects so carefully planned will be the exact opposite of what was intended. I do not need to sit in the audience or study the faces of the people, but, standing at the side of the stage, I can feel the audience's mood. The rustling of programs, coughing, the shuffling of feet—all these tell their story more plainly than words can express. Each means revision, blue-penciling, or transposition.

With time pressing and under uncomfortable conditions the play is being altered again and new shadings are given to the interpretations of the characters. As soon as the regular performance is at an end and the theatre is empty, we begin to rehearse. Parts of the play, here and there, are gone over again and again, and new methods are tried in the effort to achieve a desired effect. Sometimes these supplementary rehearsals are prolonged until the early morning hours, when my weary actors disperse to catch a little sleep before taking the train to the next city. But the date for our return has already been set and eventually we find ourselves back in New York.

If possible, I avoid holding the first performance of a new play in my New York theatres on a Monday night. Much more satisfactory results are reached by giving the members of my company a day or two to rest and recover their equilibrium. Then comes the birth—the real birth—of the play.

On the opening night I go to the theatre early. I visit my people in their dressing-rooms, trying, when possible, to chat on subjects not connected with the play, but, when necessary, reminding them and cautioning them of little touches, here and there, in their work. They are all on their mettle, of course, and I know from our weeks of association and labor that they are as anxious for the success of the play as I.

During the performance I never sit in the audience, but stand in the entrances to the stage—watching, directing, trying to quiet nervousness and to inspire confidence. I constantly tell my people of reports that I have heard from the front of the theatre, though really I have heard nothing, for I cut myself off completely from the first-night audience. While the performance is in progress I never reprove, no matter what occurs, but always encourage. My actors are nothing more than emotional children—creatures of impulse—and in this grueling test I treat them as such. At last the final curtain falls. The applause ends and we hear the audience leave the theatre. We are conscious, at least, that we have all done our best, and we await the public's verdict.

Chapter III

DEVELOPING THE BEST IN THE ACTOR

I

IT is at once a disadvantage and an advantage to the dramatic producer who sets a high ideal for his work that this country, which supports the theatre more generously than any other, does not provide such a school for the training of dramatic ability as the Paris Conservatoire.

Talent must come to the American stage untutored. Since he is denied the preparatory courses of study which would be considered necessary for the successful practice of any other of the artistic professions, the actor, to a great extent, is a victim of the influences and circumstances which attend his first entrance into the theatre. His fortunes, especially in the early period of his career, are nearly always the result of accident, not of discipline. That is why personality counts for so much on our stage to-day. It also explains why so many among even our most popular actors seem unable to progress beyond the constant performance of types of character which fall within a very limited range of technique, or are identical with their own temperaments and natures.

To the dramatic producer, who does not have the special ability to mold and develop latent talent in the actor to suit his immediate purposes, the disadvantage of these conditions in the theatre, for which there seems to be no practical remedy, is that he must accept his actors as they offer themselves to him. His ambition may have set a high standard for the work to which he gives his energies; but in the end the result will be limited by the caliber of the acting with which he is compelled to deal.

If, however, the producer have the ability to teach and develop, as well as direct; if he be able, through peculiar methods of his own, to make the actors who come under his management respond to his conception of character, the conditions in our theatre operate to his advantage. By requiring him to be on the lookout constantly for promising new material for his companies, and by forcing him to depend upon his own methods for the interpretation of characters, he is able to stamp upon all his productions, no matter how they may differ in the kinds of interest they offer, the distinguishing mark of his own individuality. To this extent he sets himself apart from the group of routine stage-managers and becomes a creative artist.

In my own experience through many years as a dramatic producer I have found it advantageous to develop by my own methods the people who have appeared in my plays. In selecting them I have always, as far as possible, given no less careful consideration to their pliability and willingness to respond to my training than to their prospective ability.

Many men and women during this time have risen to distinction in my theatres. Some, no doubt, would have succeeded as well if they had lived their careers under other influences. The peculiar qualities which are combined in the great dramatic artist must be born in him. They imply imagination and emotional faculties which are gifts of nature that cannot be transmitted or acquired. No process of training can develop histrionic genius that does not already exist in latent form. So it would not be just to the noted stars of my stages for me to assume all credit for what they have accomplished, though their development in many instances took place under my guidance.

When a young woman—or a young man—comes to me with ambitions to go on the stage, or when, from bits of acting I may have seen them do, I am convinced that they have the qualifications for success and that my interest in them will result to our mutual advantage, I can usually decide, after a very few minutes'

Lenore Ulric
One of the newest of the Belasco stars

Frances Starr

David Warfield
His most characteristic and best
personal photograph.

Mrs. Leslie Carter

Scene from Metropolitan Opera-House Production of "The
Girl of the Golden West" Which Mr. Belasco Directed When
Puccini Wrote the Operatic Score for His Play

Enrico Caruso as Ramirez, the road-agent, in the center of the picture.
At right of Caruso are Emmy Destinn as The Girl and Pasquale Amato
as Jack Rance, the gambler-sheriff

conversation, in what direction their best possibilities lie. I try to determine their views of life and what have been their experiences with life. This attitude toward the world around them is likely to dictate whether they are best suited to comedy or serious drama, to rôles of humorous or emotional interest. I do not ask that they talk much to me; I prefer to talk to them, and as I talk I watch their eyes.

Through the eyes of a listener I can form a truer judgment of his emotional capacity and imaginative faculty than in any other way. The power to listen well on the part of an actor or actress has a greater effect upon the heart and imagination of an audience than any words written by a poet. I have always found that the men and women who have come under my direction and listened well with their eyes have invariably been the ones who have climbed to the heights of their profession.

When I have discovered the aptitude for which I have been looking, the slow processes of the training then begin. It would be an easy task for the stage director, if he could find a common denominator among all the people who come under his control. Then he could follow a set method in developing the best that is in them. But no two people can be taught alike. The means which must be followed to bring about the desired result must be as various as the temperaments, intelligences, and natures of the actors who are subject to them.

It is most important that the individuality of the actor, whatever be the character he is to interpret, be preserved, for individuality is an essential qualification of a great artist. So, at the outset, I suggest little to my people, in order to make them suggest more. I appeal to their imagination, emotion, and intelligence, and draw from them all I can. When I can get no more from them, I then give them all there is in me. I coax and cajole, or bulldoze and torment, according to the temperament with which I have to deal.

A good many years ago—the calendar has changed more than twenty times since then—the literal description I was compelled to give, in a lawsuit, of the means by which I developed Mrs. Leslie Carter until she became an eminent emotional star was misconstrued, not by the court, but in the published accounts of the proceedings, until the popular impression gained of my methods as a dramatic producer was that I was a veritable Bluebeard of the theatre. I was pictured as a relentless monster who tyrannized over the hapless actors who fell into my clutches and brought out the latent ability in them by sheer brute force.

Mrs. Carter was then rising rapidly to the place of great distinction she afterward attained as a star under my guidance. The humorous writers represented me as having mauled my frail victim with fiendishly calculated brutality. One of the favorite beliefs held of me was that I dragged her around by the hair and savagely beat her head against the scenery in my effort to stimulate her emotional fervor. The fact that one of Mrs. Carter's physical glories was her bright-red hair helped to make this alleged phase of my training of her the more picturesque.

These stories did not end with the newspaper reports of the lawsuit. They became an inspiration to fiction-writers, who used them in stories; and sometimes, to my great amusement, they have even found their way back to me in the form of sensational episodes in the plays of amateur dramatists.

It is always too bad to spoil a good story. But I must do so now for the first time, because what I was misunderstood to say in my testimony at the lawsuit was, in fact, one of the most important details in the process of Mrs. Carter's development under my training.

When she came to me, fired with a determination to become a great actress, and I decided to undertake her stage education, my first step was to turn Mrs. Carter over to the care of a doctor and a physical instructor. She had been passing through a distracting domestic crisis and was both bodily and nervously run down. I outlined a systematic course of callisthenic and dancing exercises, which I had her follow for the cultivation of grace and repose. To help build up her vitality and strengthen her lungs I made her take long walks daily, which are conducive to good health and bright eyes.

For months I kept her at this physical training. Although she was most conscientious in following my formula, she could not understand what such things had to do with acting on the stage. When her strength returned, I arranged a carefully laid-out plan of vocal instruction and gradually her breathing, enunciation, and the placing of her voice were corrected and improved. I had observed that she was a very nervous woman, given to too much facial expression, so I kept her at physical exercises until this dangerous fault was overcome.

Weeks lengthened into months and still Mrs. Carter, who followed a routine that filled almost the entire day, was not permitted to try to act. When, finally, she began to get her voice under control I set her to work memorizing short poems and simple one-act plays, such as "The Happy Pair" and "The Conjugal Lesson." Then I observed that, though she was at ease in any drawing-room, she became restrained, clumsy, and uncertain the moment she stepped out on the stage. She was also afraid of the sound of her own voice, which is always disturbing at first to any new actress. So I had her read aloud each day for hours until she grew accustomed to hear herself speak.

Nearly a year elapsed while Mrs. Carter, with a willingness and persistency which showed how great was her determination to become an actress, kept at this preliminary and not very interesting routine. Then arrived the time when she was ready to begin the actual work of stage training and I commenced to lead her into the art of impersonation by drilling her in selected scenes from standard plays. I knew she was an enthusiastic horse-woman, so I gave her the speech in which Lady Gay Spanker describes the race in "London Assurance," which proved useful because it required rapid enunciation under stress of enthusiasm.

To develop her in the formal mood of classical comedy, I had her learn and act whole scenes from "She Stoops to Conquer," and to teach her to control her emotional ability, which she possessed from the first, I drilled her over and over again in the tearful parting scene between Father Duval and Marguerite in "Camille." Then she became proficient in the sleep-walking scene from "Macbeth," which is important to the training of any actress, for there is no better way to gain control of the face, body, and eyes.

Meanwhile I directed that Mrs. Carter repeat aloud four times every day the Second Player's Speech from the third act of "Hamlet." In the whole range of the English classic drama there is no passage which offers so many difficulties to clear enunciation and right diction as these six lines, which run:

Thoughts black, hands apt, drugs fit, and time agreeing;
Confederate season, else no creature seeing;
Thou mixture rank, of midnight weeds collected,
With Hecate's ban thrice blasted, thrice infected
Thy natural magic and dire property
On wholesome life usurp immediately.

The actor who can speak this complexly worded speech "trippingly on the tongue," as Hamlet puts it, has mastered one of the greatest intricacies of the English language. I have discovered few in my whole professional experience who were equal to it; yet so industrious was Mrs. Carter that she was soon able to give it with perfect clarity in a dozen different moods.

This process went on for months. To stimulate her vivacity Mrs. Carter learned from end to end the rôle of Cyprienne in Sardou's "Divorçons," and to cultivate the tremendous outbursts of passion which, as her development progressed, I became more and more convinced were eventually to become her forte as an actress, I drilled her in the violent curse scene from "Leah, the Forsaken." By this time she had acquired sufficient technique to utilize to best advantage all her natural gifts of imagination and emotion. Even in an empty theatre, without that nervous exhilaration produced by an audience's presence, she became so tremendous in this passage from the old play that she reminded me vividly of Clara Morris at her best.

It was in my effort to drill Mrs. Carter in sudden transitions of intense emotions that I hit upon a scene which, when I afterward described it in court, made me appear as a ferocious monster who would stop at no limit of physical violence to compel my actresses to do my bidding. In the whole range of modern melodrama there is no episode quite so grisly and awe-compelling as the one in "Oliver Twist," in which the infuriated Bill Sykes beats to death the faithful Nancy.

I secured a dramatization of Dickens's novel, and in our rehearsals I impersonated Bill, while Mrs. Carter, of course, represented Nancy. In outlining the realism of the murder scene in the lawsuit I related how Bill Sykes dragged the woman by the hair and beat her head against the wall and furniture. The recital proved too great a temptation to the court reporters. In the newspapers next morning I read with amusement, not unmixed with chagrin, how I had confessed to stimulating Mrs. Carter's artistic resources by resorting to the methods of the caveman. Perhaps it is unfortunate to explode at this late day a bit of favorite fiction of the journalistic humorists, but the truth should be told, nevertheless, in the story of Mrs. Carter's preparation to tread the theatre's path to fame.

There are thousands of young women who turn to the stage in the mistaken belief that it is an easy, quick, and pleasant way to success. I advise them all to consider carefully the study and preparation Mrs. Carter underwent in order to make possible her first successful appearance in public in a comparatively simple play. For two whole years, alone in her apartment, in my studio, and on the barren stages of empty theatres, she worked almost incessantly. Every phase of her training, even to the minutest details, I devised and superintended. Every step she took was with my guidance. At the end of that time the foundation of her splendid equipment as an emotional star had been laid, and she had become the mistress of thirty widely contrasted, difficult rôles, any one of which she could have played at two hours' notice.

Mrs. Carter's exceptional achievement was the result of gradual and systematic development. Until she had acquired great proficiency as an artist and had established herself with her public I was careful not to have her appear in characters which were out of harmony with her own nature and temperament.

II

It is when actors are rigid and fixed in their methods, especially when they are of foreign nationalities, that the stage director meets with the greatest difficulty in counteracting their temperamental peculiarities and bending them to his will. I found out how great this difficulty is, and what tact and patience are needed to overcome it, when, in 1911, I directed at the Metropolitan Opera House the dramatic part of the production of my own "Girl of the Golden West" which the Italian composer, Puccini, made into a grand opera. I had never before drilled an operatic company and I set about the task with a good many misgivings. The chorus of more than one hundred people was made up of Italians, French, Germans, Bohemians, and Poles. They were all inclined to gesticulate violently and to act with other characteristically foreign traits, each after the manner of his own country.

Among the group of Metropolitan stars was only one native American. Of the rest—I shall refer to their characters by the names used in my original dramatic version of the play—Enrico Caruso, who sang the rôle of Dick Johnson, the Stranger, is an Italian;

Pasquale Amato, who was cast as Jack Rance, the gambler and Sheriff, is also an Italian, and Emmy Destinn, who impersonated the title character, the Girl, is a Bohemian.

It was necessary to harmonize this incongruous collection of nationalities and make them appear as Western gold-miners—to create through them an atmosphere of the wild Californian days of 1849. I was much in doubt whether grand-opera singers who commanded princely salaries and were accustomed to special prerogatives unknown in the dramatic profession would be willing to submit to my dictation.

I soon discovered my doubts had been without foundation. The task of making the production was quite as great as I expected, but never before had I dealt with a more tractable and willing company of stage people. I was always put to the disadvantage of not understanding their languages, and very few of them could speak mine. Yet in a short time I was able to communicate my wishes through pantomime and they seemed to comprehend me at once.

I do not think that ever before in the theatre the value of pantomime and facial expression was so conclusively proved, for by this method I found I could appeal to the intelligence and imagination of this polyglot assemblage more clearly and forcibly than by words. In the

end I accomplished all I had undertaken.
Both the critics and public agreed that never
before had Metropolitan singers been so restful, so thoroughly in the spirit of the characters
they represented, and so alive to the purely
dramatic demands of a grand-opera production.

At the first rehearsal of the chorus I discovered it would be necessary to change my
stage - directing methods. Men and women
by the scores and fifties would troop out on
the stage, range themselves in rows, and become
merely a background for the principals. Then,
for no clear purpose, they would all begin to
shrug their shoulders, grimace, and gesticulate
with their hands. I resolved to undo all this
at once. I located the ones who shrugged too
much and either backed them up against
trees and rocks or invented bits of "business"
by which they were held by the others. When
a chorus-singer became incorrigible in the use
of his arms I made him go through entire scenes
with his hands in his pockets. Little by little I
tamed this wriggling crowd until they themselves began to understand the value of repose.

To form some idea how the stars intended
to interpret their rôles, I allowed them to go
through the first rehearsal almost undirected.
I found that, according to the convention of
grand opera, they would step to the front of the
stage and sing the music allotted to them with
very little effort to impersonate character,

always using the scenery merely as a background. I wondered what the revolt would be when I let them know I intended to do away with all such formalities and introduce the absolute "business" of the play, even if it were necessary for them to sing with their backs turned to the audience.

I was relieved when all of them promised to attempt the innovation, though they seemed dubious as to how my plans would work out. So I put Emmy Destinn behind the bar of the Polka Saloon and directed her to sing while she was serving drinks to the miners. It was hard for her to adapt herself to this byplay, which took place far back on the stage, for she had to readjust her voice to the new distances, but she soon succeeded.

Meanwhile I was wondering how Caruso would comply with my orders. In the first scene he had to stride into the Polka Saloon, fling his saddle on the table, and call for drinks, and with his back to the audience sing his opening song. He was entirely willing to adopt this method of making his entrance, although he must have realized it would prevent him from acknowledging the applause which invariably greets him. Later, when, wounded, after leaving the cabin of the Girl, he staggers back inside and climbs the steep ladder to the cabin loft, meanwhile singing all the time, Caruso seemed a little reluctant.

"It is difficult, for I must sing," he said, shrugging his shoulders.

"But even if Puccini has given you a song at just this point, you must suit the words to the action and the action to the words," I explained.

"Let me see you do it," he replied.

So I pretended I was Dick Johnson, staggered in with my wound, listened to the approach of the Sheriff's posse, and then climbed up the ladder, singing in a voice that must have made the very walls of the Metropolitan groan with agony.

Caruso saw the value of the realism in a flash. A dozen or more times at each rehearsal after that, in response to my directions, he would go through the scene and end by climbing up the ladder, all the time pouring forth tenor notes which were worth bagsful of gold. He was full of enthusiasm and was not content until he could play the scene as well as could reasonably have been expected of any accomplished actor on the dramatic stage. The prodigious amount of wasted song he poured into the dark recesses of the big, empty Metropolitan, as he good-naturedly toiled up and down the almost perpendicular ladder during these long rehearsals, would have sent his worshiping public into transports of delight.

I had more misgivings over the melodramatic scene in which the Girl, when she is insulted by the Sheriff, seizes a whisky-bottle to defend herself. Puccini, probably without considering the dramatic necessities of the situation, had given Emmy Destinn a very difficult aria to accompany it. I wondered what would happen when I had to tell her that, in order to carry out my conception of the realism of the scene, she would have to sing and struggle at the same time. I knew it was contrary to all the traditions of the grand-opera stage. I also was not unaware of the temperamental idiosyncrasies of grand-opera stars when they are asked to change their established methods. So I was the more surprised and delighted to find her keen to adopt every suggestion I made.

In the rehearsals I would take the part of the Sheriff and she, as the Girl, would beat and scratch me until my face and body bore the marks of her realism. After three or four trials she acted it so vividly that even the few people who were watching the rehearsals would break into applause.

When I originally produced "The Girl of the Golden West" in my own New York theatre I found the gambling scene, in which the Girl takes a playing-card from her stocking, to be the most difficult I had ever rehearsed with a dramatic company. To keep the audience in the right state of suspense needed the most skilled acting by Blanche Bates,

Robert Hilliard, and Frank Keenan, who then impersonated the rôles. It can be understood how very much harder the scene became with Destinn, Caruso, and Amato in the characters. It must have been exceedingly trying to them to change abruptly the operatic technique which had become almost second nature to them. But they seemed actually to enjoy making the experiment. Over and over again they would go through the episode until they completely conquered it. These geniuses received a fortune every time they appeared in public, but they gave me many-fold at my bidding. All the while Toscanini was scolding them from the conductor's stand and making them repeat the music. That sort of interruption was also new to me, but, somehow, we always found ourselves in perfect sympathy, he directing the music and I creating the atmosphere and evolving the drama.

To have directed the grand-opera version of my play with these famous singers in the cast was one of the most interesting, as well as one of the most instructive, experiences in my career. I came to realize better than ever before how necessary are heart, soul, intelligence, and imagination to the lyric artist. Only the greatest singers of the past and present have possessed these four supreme qualities. Every singer, however great his lyric gift, should be taught—indeed, should be made—to act. Even Caruso's God-given voice casts a more potent spell over his audiences in the ratio that he improves as an actor. The fact that so many inferior singers succeed when so many better singers fail is not strange. It is because they have greater imaginations and more understanding hearts. The secret of the marvelous influence of Mary Garden, Emma Calvé, Geraldine Farrar, and Maurice Renaud over their hearers is that these singers know how to appeal to the imaginations of their public through their own imaginations. It is no less true of the concert stage. John McCormack, standing alone on a platform, is equally able to stir the imagination of his hearers. If nature had denied any of these geniuses a singing voice, all would still have become great actors or actresses.

I do not know how the dramatic realism which we put into "The Girl of the Golden West" was preserved when the opera settled back into the regular *répertoire*, but to me its early performances were closer to life and nature than any other grand opera I have ever witnessed. I am glad to have directed the dramatic side of the production at the Metropolitan, for it taught me that the deities of the world of song are not the eccentric creatures they are so often represented to be, but sensible, obliging, and companionable men and women.

It was the wealth of imagination I detected in Frances Starr's acting the first time I saw her that convinced me at once of the possibilities in store for her, if she were properly directed. When I made up my mind to invite her into my company, I felt sure I could place her among the stars if only she would prove strong enough, physically, for the struggle. I understood much better than she what effort it would cost, what trying experiences were ahead of her. She was a frail girl, with a highly strung, nervous temperament, and I decided that what she needed most at the outset was to be built up in health. As a result of my first interview with her after her contract had been signed, I instructed her to consult a physician and engage a trained nurse. When I told her I must insist upon prescribing her diet and regulating her physical exercise, she was inclined at first to resent interference in her personal affairs. Quite naturally, she had supposed that my only requirement of her would be to act. But when I explained the long rehearsals that are preliminary to my productions and showed her the need of a sound physical foundation for the nervous energy I would require her to exert, she began to appreciate better the wisdom of my suggestions. For many weeks all I asked her to do was to eat nutritious food, drink milk, take daily exercise in the open air, and go to bed early. This was actually the beginning of the making of Miss Starr into the splendid actress she has since become.

When, after a time in David Warfield's company, she appeared in the romantic character of the Spanish girl in "The Rose of the Rancho," she so completely fulfilled all my expectations that I was certain she would give a brilliant account of herself in rôles demanding intense emotionalism, if only I could contrive somehow to stir her imagination to an even higher pitch.

The opportunity came when Eugene Walter wrote "The Easiest Way" for me. In it he had drawn, in the character of Laura Murdock, one of those unfortunate women who wish to live in luxury on nothing a week—a pitifully weak, unmoral, constitutionally mendacious creature who drifts to perdition along the path of least resistance. Mr. Walter had created this vivid and truthful, though thoroughly unsympathetic, character with a view to having Charlotte Walker impersonate it, and he was quite insistent that the part be given to her. But as I studied it, the peculiar qualities which I felt sure Frances Starr could impart to it were always before my eyes and I made up my mind to intrust it to her.

J. was not mistaken. It was "The Easiest Way" and its character of Laura Murdock which proved to be the making of Miss Starr

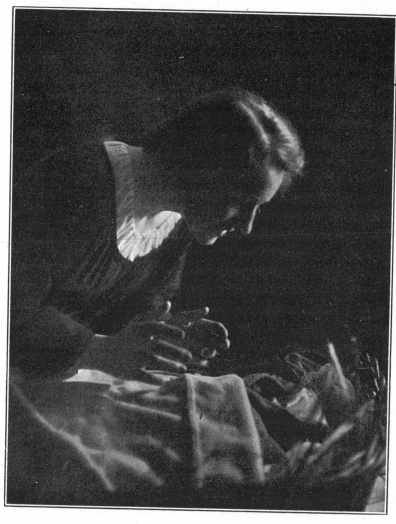

Frances Starr in the Final Act of "Marie-Odile"
by Edward Knoblock

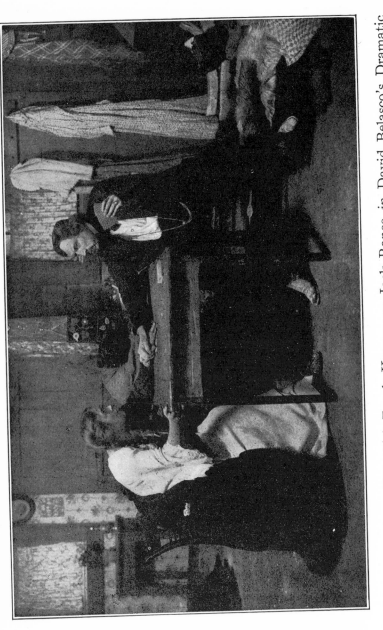

Blanche Bates as The Girl, Frank Keenan as Jack Rance, in David Belasco's Dramatic Production of "The Girl of the Golden West," in 1905

into a really fine actress. But it made necessary at least one experience which not only she and I, but the rest of the company, are not likely to forget. If the means by which I cultivated emotionalism in Mrs. Carter could be misconstrued as a resort to physical violence, the course I was forced to take with Miss Starr might much more correctly be called mental torment.

She had met all my requirements up to the climax of the play. At this point came the situation, at once grisly, abject, and pitiful, in which the weakling, a victim of her own mendacity, and abandoned by the man who trusted her, seizes a pistol with the intention of killing herself, but lacks the courage and, with a shriek of terror, throws the weapon down. I had foreseen that this episode must be worked up to the highest possible pitch of frenzied hysteria.

It proved too great an effort for Miss Starr, who, though we rehearsed it scores of times, could never muster the strength for it. It was not a moment when facial pantomime or "frozen emotion" would produce the right thrill. What I wanted was a scream which would denote a soul in torment, the abject terror of a little weakling whose life had been wasted in careless pursuit of gay things and who suddenly found herself brought face to face with death. Such a moment Mrs. Carter had once wonderfully expressed when, as Madame Du Barry, she listened to her jailer read the warrant for her execution.

I was at a loss for a long time how to make Miss Starr respond to the requirements of the scene. Then I saw it would be necessary to be harsh, to torment the little girl, and, by humiliating her before the company, to drive her to the point of hysterics. I was sure, if only once I could force her up to the pitch of frenzy which the scene demanded, that she would be able to master it and repeat it. We went over it again and again while the rest of the company looked on in silent anger. Miss Starr was trembling and as white as a ghost as, little by little, I drove her to desperation. At each attempt she still fell short. Then I remembered she often had told me how she idolized Sarah Bernhardt, so I resolved to taunt her.

"And you want to be as great as Bernhardt!" I sneered. "It makes me laugh!"

In a flash Miss Starr gave a terrific scream and dropped to the floor of the stage in a dead faint. As those nearest to her lifted her up, I clapped my hands and said:

"That's what I want! That's exactly what I've been working for these last three hours!"

Then I dismissed the rehearsal. The company walked out of the theatre without even bidding me good night. Every member was fairly exploding with resentment. Miss Starr's sister, who happened to be present, took charge of her and sent her home in a cab. I was glad when they had gone. I wanted to be alone, for I had accomplished a successful but most distasteful afternoon's work.

About two hours afterward the sister called me on the telephone, saying Miss Starr was more composed and wanted to see me. I lost no time in going to her apartment. The first words she said were:

"I think I made an awful fool of myself at the rehearsal. But I just couldn't do what you wanted."

She was still very much frightened and in doubt.

"On the contrary, you did exactly what I wanted you to do," I replied. "I knew it was in you, and I was sure you could do it."

Then I told her that when we rehearsed the scene again I would expect the same scream she had given that afternoon.

"I don't think I can ever do it again that way," she replied.

"All right," said I, "if you don't, then you will have to go through the whole thing again."

"No! No!" she cried. "I just couldn't!"

"Then scream," I said.

"Well," said Miss Starr, "I'll try."

When the next rehearsal was called I still had doubts as to what the result might be.

But Miss Starr rose to the climax of the scene with perfect ease.

Two months later, when "The Easiest Way" was produced in my New York theatre, I watched the effect of Laura Murdock's frenzied scream upon the audience. The tense suspense, followed by the burst of applause, eased the pricking of my conscience for having tormented Miss Starr to the point of hysterics, for it became really the starting-point of her march to great success.

III

A stage-manager cannot dispassionately explain to his people, especially to the players of limited experience, how he wants them to act, and expect them to throw their whole soul and being into it. He must first, himself, definitely imagine every scene in which they appear, and then lead them up to it by working upon their intelligence, imagination, and feeling.

I have reached this general conclusion after much experience in the development of actors. But it is also true that no two can be taught alike, just as it is impossible to produce any two plays by following the same set rules. There may arise instances in which the most vivid and impressive effects of character can best be secured by adopting a negative method of projecting it. Such examples are few, but one, at least, is afforded by my production of "The Return of Peter Grimm."

My purpose in this play was to show, in the person of a living actor, the survival of the influence of a powerful personality after death. In other words, it was to become the difficult task of David Warfield, for whom the character was written, to impersonate not an animate being, but a ghost, or shade. I never had any doubt of Mr. Warfield's ability to perform his share in carrying out my conception of the character. An actor of his intelligence and technical resources could scarcely fail. The difficulty of my problem lay in what would be the attitude of the surrounding characters toward a commanding personage who was never to be seen or heard, but whose presence was always felt. I foresaw that, in impersonating Peter Grimm, no matter how convincing Mr. Warfield's acting might be, the conviction which the character must ultimately carry to the audience would depend upon the acting of those around it.

In the writing of the play I had trouble from the very start. To make old Peter's character clearly understood, it was necessary that he be represented in life through at least one act. The dramatic conflict of the story, however, had to come in the two succeeding acts, when he must be kept on the stage constantly in spirit form. It would have been comparatively easy, of course, to sustain such an illusion for only five or ten minutes. At a time when the public was less sophisticated in matters of the theatre than it is to-day it might have been possible to heighten an illusion of ghostliness by the aid of suggestive lights. Here, though, was a case in which an audience was given two hours in which to analyze the character. If, even for a moment, it failed to suggest death—if, for so much as a single second, it appealed to a sense of the ridiculous—the fate of the whole play was sealed.

I decided that the most convincing effects could be secured by employing the simplest means. First of all I had to create around the living Peter an atmosphere of memories. The house in which I revealed him was built by his ancestors of a century before—old-fashioned, quaint, and mellow, and yet with the few modern improvements which naturally would be made in such a place. The furniture, gathered by the founders of his family, had to be old and worn; the ancient clock that almost spoke as it ticked, the great fireplace, with armchair and stool before it—trifling objects, to be sure, but all of a kind that might be hallowed by recollections of the departed one. Thus I gradually evolved the environment in which it seemed to me the story could best be told.

It was then necessary to choose a nationality for Peter which harmonized with the mood of the play. I recalled the characters out of *Grimm's Fairy Tales,* "The Flying Dutchman," "Rip Van Winkle," and other beautiful, fanciful figures of fiction, and decided he would be most appealing if I represented him as Dutch. To give him a profession in life I considered many things. I wanted him to symbolize one who had loved life and had lived in the midst of growing things, so I made him a gardener who had come from a family of gardeners.

All these traits in Peter Grimm's nature I emphasized in the opening act, in which he was represented in the flesh. Then he sat down in his old armchair before the fire, and when the family came to arouse him to go to bed, they found him dead.

Now came the hard task of reincarnating Peter in spirit form, when he returns to repair the mistake he made in life, upon which depended the happiness of those he had left behind. For weeks I pondered how it could be best contrived, and then I decided that he must walk through the same door, hang his hat on the same peg, and move across the room to the same table—just as the audience had seen him in the preceding act.

To rehearse the play up to this point and make the company indicate clearly the essential preliminary details of the story was not especially difficult. But when it came time to have a spirit form mingle with ten animate beings who always felt its influence, yet remained unaware of its actual presence, the management of the scenes became most perplexing.

The requirements placed upon Mr. Warfield were very severe. He had to imagine himself returned from the unknown world with an unfulfilled mission to perform. He could not give vent to any emotion whatever; he must typify death. When he stood for thirty-eight minutes without speaking a word as the daily life of the household went on around him, yet had to command the unwavering attention of the audience, he gave what I believe to be the greatest exhibition of acting I ever witnessed. During all this time he remained in perfect repose and with eyes fixed. When he left the scene Mr. Warfield would be in a state of utter exhaustion, and would actually have to sit ten minutes in order to bring himself, so to speak, back to life.

Sensative as was Mr. Warfield's acting, this illusion of death could not be reached or, once reached, be maintained by him alone. The ultimate effect of the character depended upon the relationship of the other characters to it. To insure this illusion I had to develop my actors along peculiar lines. They had to be taught to look at Mr. Warfield, yet not see him. They had to listen to his speeches, but indicate that they thought his voice was in their imaginations. At one point a little child had to be taught to run to him, throw his arms around him, and yet not know that he was there. Even to the least important character in the play, the actors had to be taught to indicate a negation of all the physical senses.

To accomplish all this required the most persistent practice. Every detail in the play was so perfectly timed that the movements of my actors were guided by the beat of their pulse. I drilled them until they could have circled around Mr. Warfield blindfolded, and yet not touch him. Until I came to rehearse this peculiar play I never had half realized what miracles can be performed by constant training, when a group of actors are working in perfect unison to accomplish a single purpose or illusion.

This drilling did not stop with the people on the stage. Even the scene-shifters had to undergo a course of careful instruction. I required them to wear felt slippers and had the floors covered with heavy matting so that no accidental sound would disturb the spell that had been created.

Night after night, as long as the play remained before the public, all these precautions were observed until they became very exhausting to every one concerned in the performance. But no accident of any kind occurred during the long run of the play, and I never saw a single indication from the audience that this dangerous nightly traffic with a ghost was other than seriously accepted.

There could be no better demonstration of the value of pantomime as a part of an actor's equipment than David Warfield's performance of Peter Grimm.   In all my experience in the theatre I can recall only two examples which compare with it.   One was the exalted dignity of silence which James O'Neill attained when he embodied the Saviour in my production of "The Passion Play" in San Francisco, long ago in the 'eighties.   The other occurred during Sarah Bernhardt's remarkable performance of Mary Magdalene in "The Good Samaritan." For forty-five minutes the Magdalene sat under a portico, listening to the voice of the Master as he spoke to the multitude.   During all this time she did not utter a word.   But the story of her redemption, as it was expressed in her face and by her gestures, was more eloquently and beautifully told than if it had been written in the poetry of Shakespeare.

In making my dramatic productions I have nearly always found my resources as a director put to a much harder test with actors of long experience, whose manner and method have become fixed in certain definite lines of parts, than with those, perhaps of much more limited technical proficiency, who have not gone beyond the pliable state when they are still susceptible to new methods of expression. The permanent stock companies of an earlier era of our stage have all but disappeared. In spite of the familiar arguments in their favor, the old system would no longer be found advisable. The public is fickle now, even in its attitude toward its favorites. It decrees constant change in the theatre. So dramatic companies must disband at the end of the life of a play. And, with the staging of each successive play, the producer is confronted by the necessity of assembling what is practically a new organization.

This prevailing practice in the theatre is too likely to result in robbing the work of the stage director of its individuality. The temptation becomes strong to select an actor for a certain rôle, not because he is a good actor, but because he suggests a certain type. With the present custom of producing plays in wholesale numbers, and then taking commercial advantage of a chance success by immediately duplicating it, there is little effort on the part of most stage directors to train their actors to express more than the surface aspects of the characters in which they appear.

When I adapted the French drama, "The Lily," from its original version by Pierre Wolff and Gaston Leroux, for production at my theatre, I had to find an actress of very definite type for its electrical character of Odette, and to demand that she play the part in exact accordance with my own conception of it. For two acts, although she was constantly on the stage, it was necessary that she completely efface herself. Then, in the third act, came an emotional outburst of no more than two minutes' duration which, if it were properly given, must raise the character to commanding importance in the drama. Where to find an actress of superlative emotional ability whom I could induce to abnegate herself throughout practically the whole play greatly perplexed me.

This character of Odette was an unlovely, middle-aged spinster sister in a French family, whose heart had been eaten out by her lifelong servile obedience to a domineering, selfish father, and whose doglike loyalty and affection for her younger sister, Christiane, had become her complete obsession.

Christiane, kept by her tyrannical father from marrying the man she loves, gives herself to him in desperation. On the discovery of her guilt, Odette's resentment, pent up for years, suddenly bursts all restraint as she goes to her sister's defense. The drab, abject, bullied, and neglected old maid, who never before had dared to raise her voice against her father's tyranny, is transformed in an instant from a servile, driven sheep into a savage wolf as she pours out her hatred upon him. On the ability of the actress I might select to rise to the demands of this scene depended the fate of "The Lily."

As I considered the rôle and its exceptional requirements my thoughts turned to Nance O'Neil. She possessed the tall, gaunt figure, the well-modulated contralto voice, the plain, spinster-like appearance, and the emotional tensity which I had imagined in the character. Other actresses entered my mind as I hesitated a month, but always I reverted to Miss O'Neil.

Nevertheless, I saw trouble ahead. Miss O'Neil's dramatic training had been for the heavy rôles of tragedy. She had acquired the broad gesticulation of classic character and the manner of elocution which fitted into the reading of blank verse. She had long acted successfully in different parts of the world and had broken away from all restraints of stage-management. It was plain that, in developing Miss O'Neil for the rôle of Odette, while I might have to teach her little, she herself would have to unlearn much. I was in the difficult position of expecting an actress of great experience to change abruptly all her established methods—to turn right-about-face in a single night.

I sent for her and, together, we went carefully over the play, I acting the part of Odette as I thought it ought to be played. I made her understand that until the single scene which was to become her great opportunity arrived, she must remain in complete repose. Until then her only lines would be spoken in low monosyllables. I told her that her appearance must be wholly unattractive, that her face must be colorless, pinched, and inexpressive, to typify the utter tragedy of life.

She listened in silence for a long time. Then she said:

"Repose is a thing I don't know. I haven't any confidence that I will be able to act the part as you wish. But it appeals to me, and if you have confidence in me I shall be glad to come into your company, not as a star, but as one of the players in what I believe will be a great cast. I will do everything as you direct, and try to forget I have ever acted any other kind of characters. If you are willing to take the risk, so can I."

I told her that what she said had convinced me she could make out of the drab rôle of Odette the most powerful character in the play. Without the slightest misgivings on my part the terms of our agreement were then arranged.

Some of my staff did not share my confidence in the experiment, and during the first two or three rehearsals it seemed at times that they might be right. Miss O'Neil, who for years had been the most prominent figure in all the plays in which she had appeared, found it hard to keep herself in the background of the action, and it was irritating to her to speak always in two-word sentences. It needed very diplomatic handling to lead her along my way and at the same time keep her convinced of the paramount importance of her small rôle.

But she had none of the false pride which is so common among actors who feel that they have established reputations behind them. I have known many who, though willing to listen to instructions in private, immediately grew resentful when directed or corrected in the presence of the rest of the company. Miss O'Neil had no such exaggerated ideas of her importance. Bits of the play which must have seemed trivial to her she would go through twenty times in succession if I demanded it. She not only was willing to listen to criticism, but courted it. She was highly strung, like an emotional child, and sometimes would become completely discouraged.

But at last came a rehearsal in which she completely dominated the stage. The magic of her eloquent voice in her denunciation speech, the animation which her negative character suddenly took on, held the other actors spellbound.

There could be only one effect of such a performance as hers upon an audience. On the opening night of "The Lily" the surprise at first was general that so prominent an actress should have been wasted on so trivial a rôle. Then, in sudden contrast, came the brilliant flash of histrionic lightning. Two minutes sufficed for Odette's speech. When it was ended the curtain was lifted twenty-seven times before the applause subsided, and the greatest success in Nance O'Neil's career had been won.

With the run of "The Lily" my artistic association with Miss O'Neil came to an end. But the circumstances of it have never ceased to afford me satisfaction, and I trust she looks back upon them with the same degree of pleasure. To me she typifies what receptiveness, tractability, and generosity will accomplish for the player.

The true artist in the theatre never stands still. The horizon around him constantly changes. The conditions in which he finds himself never remain the same. The standard which he sets for himself must not be allowed to decline. He approaches closest to greatness who learns to govern his art to meet every requirement of the character he is called upon to perform.

Chapter IV

THE PROBLEM OF THE CHILD ACTOR

I

AMONG the callers at my studio one afternoon was a woman who came in a state of mingled enthusiasm and anxiety. That frame of mind I am not unaccustomed to among persons with ambitions to set out on a stage career who ask my advice, or among the more confident candidates who come to seek an outlet for their real or fancied talents in my productions.

I was certain from this woman's manner that her mission must be either one or the other, so I was not a little surprised when she explained that she wanted to consult me about her child, a little girl ten years old. There was novelty in the purpose of her call and at once I became interested.

With whatever show of modesty she could assume she said that she was the very proud mother of a real prodigy. Her precocious child had developed remarkable ability in reciting. It could memorize long passages from plays without difficulty. More than that, it could perform the characters with all the fervor of a grown-up actor. If I recall correctly, stretches from "Romeo and Juliet" and "As You Like It" were in the youngster's *répertoire*, not to mention many scenes from published modern plays.

Should such a gift be permitted to remain unutilized? Ought not a place on the stage be found at once for this ten-year-old phenomenon? These were the questions I was expected to answer.

I first asked the woman if she had the means of supporting and the facilities for training her daughter as a child in ordinary circumstances is supported and trained, and she replied very positively that she had. I then inquired whether its gift was an inherited proclivity. She said she did not think so, for no one in her family had ever been connected with the theatre. In answer to questions regarding the child's physical condition, she said it had always been in the best of health.

I promptly advised this mother to put aside all thought of a juvenile theatrical career for her little girl. I urged her with much earnestness to encourage its interest in dolls and children's games, and to take care not to force its education because of its precocity. If, I suggested, its talents for reciting and acting still continued when it had reached the age of sixteen or seventeen—which secretly I had reason to doubt—there still would be time enough to develop them for use in the theatre.

The woman was plainly disappointed, and she left my studio unconvinced. I later heard she had said Mr. Belasco warned her that the stage was not a fit place for children and strongly advised that she keep her little girl away from it.

Which, I hasten to make clear, is not at all the impression I intended to give her. I was offering advice which applied only in an individual case, based on what seemed to me to be the relative advantages open to this child in its home and on the stage. She had completely misunderstood my meaning and, of course, to the disparagement of the theatre.

The difficult question of the child in its relation to the professional stage, which was so important to this mother, is much more important to the child, but in a different way. We who are in and of the theatre know that it can arrive at its best results only when it meets and solves wisely the artistic and economic problems which it creates. There are also social problems in the theatre which are raised by the people associated with it. They may safely be left to the mature members of the dramatic profession whom they directly affect. But there always remains the puzzling question of what is best for the child actor who cannot think for itself and, therefore, must be subject to conditions which it cannot change or control.

One way to settle tne question—the narrow and arbitrary way that is first likely to occur to those who consider it from a single point of view—would be to eliminate children entirely from the acting profession. That would be the way of persons who know nothing of the theatre from its inside or of the actual conditions which surround the child actor. If it were the right way it would have been accomplished long ago, for the child who works in any profession or trade has never been without aggressive guardians of its welfare. On the contrary, a child's right to appear on the stage, under proper conditions and restrictions, has generally been conceded, and those who know most about its work and the influences around it agree that, relatively, it is better off in the theatre than under the conditions and influences from which more than 90 per cent. of young stage children are drawn. I am making a sharp distinction, of course, between children who appear in legitimate plays and those engaged in such hazardous or exhausting work as acrobatic exhibitions or dancing.

Although it must be a secondary argument —for the child actor must always be entitled to first consideration on the score of its health, morals, and education—the welfare of dramatic art depends to a very considerable degree upon the child performer. Children are necessary to the stage. It cannot get along without them. Many of the greatest masterpieces of dramatic literature have turned directly upon the presence and effect of little children in their scenes. The play throughout the theatre's whole history that has been most profound and universal in its appeal has dealt simply with that most enduring and powerful of all instincts—mother-love.

This motive of drama which remains supreme in contemporary works of the stage was equally common to the drama of the ancient Greeks. The tragic grief of the Queen Mother in the "Medea" of Euripides could be developed into blinding passion only by the presence in the play of her children, whom she kills to save from the woman for whom the King has betrayed and abandoned her. Shakespeare often depended upon child characters to give power and beauty to his plays. Among many examples are the rôles of Prince Arthur in "King John," the little Prince of Wales in "Richard III," and the fairies and sprites in "A Midsummer Night's Dream." "Uncle Tom's Cabin" might not have swayed millions as it did, save for the pathetic character of Little Eva.

It was the same overwhelming motive of mother-love, and the appearance of the two children in its scenes, that made a place in theatrical history for "East Lynne." In my own play, "The Return of Peter Grimm," I was obliged to introduce the character of the little boy, William, in order to have my audiences comprehend fully the tender, lovable nature of old Peter. Drama that truthfully reflects life requires the use of child actors. Only in plays that view life flippantly and cynically are they ignored. One does not find child characters in the comedies of George Bernard Shaw.

Yet it is not safe to argue, because the child actor is necessary to the theatre, that the theatre is necessary to the child. It surely is not necessary, and it offers no benefit to the child who has the ordinary advantages of comfortable home surroundings and careful parental discipline. I am by no means certain, even when a child shows great precocity for acting, that to place it in the theatre at a tender age is the best way to develop its character or cultivate its talents for future use. My own way would be to supervise with greatest care its health and education under domestic influences, and then give it a later start on the stage. If I had a child and it wanted to go into the theatre, I would question only my ability to support and train it in the home.

I do not want my views on the subject to be misunderstood. They do not imply that I

David Belasco with the Children of the "Daddies" Company at Luncheon in the Belasco Theatre Greenroom During Rehearsals

"The Return of Peter Grimm"

consider the theatre an improper place for a very large percentage of the hundreds of children who at all times are in it. The question depends altogether on what advantages the child would have received if it had remained entirely among domestic surroundings.

A distinction should also be drawn between children who come of parents belonging to the acting profession and those who are brought into the theatre from other classes and walks of life. In the case of the first, they are subject to the same influences they would probably find at home. They are also under the care of their natural guardians, who, presumably, have decided what is best for them.

In this country children on the stage who belong to theatrical families are not very numerous—at least, there are not enough of them to influence any general conclusions on the problem of the stage child. In this respect our native branch of the dramatic profession is radically different from the English, where for generations acting has been followed as a family profession.

Nevertheless, there are a few conspicuous examples in our own theatre of actors' children who have been on the stage almost from infancy and have remained there all their lives, some to win distinction in their mature years. Consider what the theatre would have lost if the right to it had been denied Maude Adams.

She was carried on at the age of seven months by her mother in "The Lost Child" and had developed genuine talent before she could speak her lines without a lisp.

Fritz Williams, also of stage parents, was only six months old when he was before the footlights of a Boston theatre in "Seeing Warren." Wallace Eddinger, who was to become a famous little Cedric in "Little Lord Fauntleroy," was a child actor at seven years, in a piece called "Among the Pines." George M. Cohan, now one of the real geniuses of our theatre, first appeared at the age of ten, in "Peck's Bad Boy." William Collier, exceedingly clever among our present farcical stars, began when he was only one year older. Holbrook Blinn was only six when he was a boy actor in "The Streets of London," though his actress mother wisely took him out of the theatre and gave him a college education. Henry B. Warner was seven years old when his celebrated father permitted him to play a child rôle, also in "The Streets of London." Fay Templeton at three was a Cupid in a spectacular play, and a year later was Puck in a New York production ot "A Midsummer Night's Dream." Maude Fealy began at three, and Phyllis Rankin at ten—both under the guidance of their parents. But the talented children of the Drews, Barrymores, and Jeffersons—the most noted professional families we have in the American theatre—like the Irvings in England, were kept off the stage until their education had been acquired.

These child actors I have named gravitated naturally to the theatre because their parents were members of its profession. Among our grown actors of repute there are some who also began as children, but without inherited aptitude for the art. Notable among them is Lotta Crabtree, now retired, who began acting at eleven in California during the gold days. Mrs. Fiske has been in the theatre practically all her life. At three she was the infant Duke of York in "Richard III"; at ten she was appearing with J. K. Emmett, at Wallack's in New York, as Little Fritz in "Fritz, Our German Cousin." She performed an astonishing number of children's rôles, and was a full-fledged star in "Fogg's Ferry" at seventeen. Louis Mann, our popular dialect star, also saw the footlights at three. Julia Marlowe began at twelve, but was taken off the stage to undergo arduous private training before she emerged as a star of poetic drama at seventeen.

Clara Morris, one of the greatest emotional stars our stage has produced, appeared at thirteen, in "The Seven Sisters," in Cleveland, though it was eleven years later that she found her *métier* as Anne Sylvester in "Men and Women" under Augustin Daly at the old Fifth Avenue Theatre. Annie Russell acted at eight. She was one of the innumerable children who have appeared in "Miss Multon," which is a version of "East Lynne." Elsie Janis, exceedingly talented as an entertainer along vaudeville lines, began in my own play, "The Charity Ball," at the tender age of eight. Edna May was lisping to audiences at five, but in amateur theatricals. Effie Shannon was a child actress in the companies controlled by the Boston manager, John Stetson. Henry E. Dixey, at ten, was the boy, Peanuts, in Augustin Daly's play, "Under the Gaslights," at the old Howard Athenæum Theatre during its first Boston run. Ada Rehan, for whom future fame was waiting, first played at fourteen in "Across the Continent," one of the very popular melodramas of its day. Julia Arthur, also at fourteen, was another of the many children who made a beginning as the little Prince of Wales in "Richard III."

I have not attempted to make a complete list of the actors and actresses, familiar to our playgoing public now, who began their stage work in infancy or very early childhood. A careful search through the native theatre would doubtless discover a good many more than I have named. Yet even in their aggregate they would form a very small fraction of the whole present membership of our stage profession. They are the fortunate ones— the few exceptions among almost innumerable child actors who have attracted no special attention, earned no distinction, and eventually dropped out of sight, to be heard of no more.

My opinion that the theatre is not an advisable place for the children of parents who are capable of bringing them up under the advantages that are normally found in the domestic circle should not be accepted as applying to the very great majority of the child actors who everywhere amuse us and appeal to our hearts. These children almost invariably come from a very humble class. Except in the occasional instances when their parents belong to the theatrical profession, we never get the children of affluence or even of the modestly well-to-do. They are of the lowliest origin—little dependents of a crippled father or a widowed mother who has had to turn to scrubbing as a precarious support for her family. Perhaps they are orphans who have been left in half-neglect while an older brother or sister is away from home at work.

The employment of such a child as this— even if, in the case of an infant, it is carried on and off the stage only once or twice during a performance—may enable a mother to support in fair comfort a family of five or six. If it happens to be a little older, the hour or two it spends in the theatre, at work which, to it, does not seem like work, is infinitely less harmful than the time it would otherwise have to spend in a dirty tenement, an ill-ventilated sweat-shop, or perhaps unlooked after in the streets.

Such children are paid from $25 to $75 a week. They very seldom receive less than the first sum. So it may be seen that they are able to earn from three to seven times more than their parents. They must be kept clean and well fed. Often they are brought for the first time in their little lives under the influence of the gospel of soap, water, and sunshine. It has been my experience that they improve at once under the changed conditions which the theatre provides. Everything is furnished for them. In many instances even their food is provided. They are never left to their own resources, for the parent or guardian is expected to be on hand always to look after them. When a play goes on the road it is always made possible for her to earn her expenses by securing employment as maid to one of the actresses in the company.

I know there is sometimes an impression that children on the stage, like Toby Tyler who ran away with the circus in the old story, are pathetic victims of neglect. But the exact opposite is more likely to be the case. They stand in greater danger of being spoiled by too much attention and petting. Selfish motives, without reference to humane considerations, dictate that a manager safeguard carefully the child who happens to be in his company, for in its welfare lies his own material advantage.

A little child is always a good influence in a theatrical company. It becomes at once an object of general interest and solicitude, the more so because actors and actresses, as a rule, live lonely lives. Its effect is to elevate the tone of the organization, for all men and women are quite sure to be careful in the presence of a child. I know of no more effectual check on the deportment of people behind the scenes of a theatre than the thought that they are being watched by wide-open, wondering eyes. Our tiny players may sometimes be a source of a good deal of trouble to us, but in this respect they furnish substantial compensation.

II

The aspect of the problem of the child actor that I have been considering up to this point has been restricted to children in a very tender period of their lives—that is, children under eight or ten years of age. In the case of boys and girls beyond that age the question becomes more difficult and complicated, for then the matter of education and discipline begins to have an important bearing on it.

But again must be borne in mind the conditions which a child of very humble origin finds in the theatre, and what that same child would be likely to encounter outside it. A theatre manager or producer of plays cannot be expected to superintend the education of the child whom he employs in his company. The most that can be asked of him is that he provide adequately for its comfort, and that he regulate its hours of rehearsal—its regular performances are an arbitrary matter— so that it will be given reasonable opportunity for study, play, and rest. The working-hours, except during the period of preliminary rehearsals, are, I may say, never long, and the work itself is more like play to the child. It loves to rehearse and to act. In fact, I have never known a child to become tired of playing its part, and I have found that it is less likely than grown actors to become careless or inattentive. The severest reproof that can be given a child actor is to deprive it a night or two from acting its rôle.

There is, as a rule, ample time for a child in a theatrical company, except on Wednesdays, which is the established midweek matinée day, to attend to study, provided the proper discipline is exercised by its parent or by the person who happens to have it in charge. If the parent is inclined to be lax in these matters of discipline, the child would be just as badly off if it were not in the theatre.

Each state also has its laws which regulate the employment and dictate the education of children, and especially in the case of the child actor these laws are rigidly enforced. I would not want to be understood as not favoring regulations which widely operate in the interest of children, especially children who for one reason or another have been deprived of the protection and guidance of parents. But when account is taken of the thousands of ragged, ill-fed, and almost abandoned children, who by day and night swarm the streets of every large city, I am led to the belief that some of our authorities and charitable societies are inclined to be over-solicitous concerning the welfare of children who find clean and pleasant employment in our theatres.

Many a time I have watched the grimy little merchants who flock around the back doors of the big newspaper offices at midnight, in heat or rain or cold, waiting for the bundles of papers, from which they can make, at best, only about a dollar profit. I have wondered who feeds them, who washes them, who cares when they come home. Then I have contrasted them with the clean, well-fed children who come and go through the stage entrance of a theatre, and I have never hesitated in my opinion as to which are the better off. And it should not be forgotten that these two groups of children come from pretty much the same class. Have the objectors on principle to the employment of children on the stage ever walked late in the evening through one of the streets of New York's lower East Side, with its dense throngs of juvenile humanity? I wonder!

If the laws which affect the employment of children on the stage were made uniform in the various states, great advantages would follow, both for the children and for the theatrical manager. Certain states, such as Massachusetts, Illinois, Maryland, and Ohio, have very drastic regulations. They prohibit the appearance on the public stage of any child under the age of sixteen. Other states, such as New York, Pennsylvania, and many more, allow them to appear in stage plays, but with restrictions as to work that might be physically injurious. Presumably, the authorities in all these states have made careful investigations before writing on their statute-books the laws which govern the work of professional children. If so, is it more harmful to a child to appear in the theatre in Massachusetts or Illinois than in the state of New York? And why?

I do not believe any theatrical manager would argue for laxity in the laws which safeguard the well-being of child actors. But all managers would prefer to have such laws standardized. A dramatic production is a delicate work of art, which is brought to perfection only after infinite thought, care, and preparation. The various elements which compose it cannot be changed without throwing its intricate machinery out of gear. All plays are eventually sent on tour, and, once having conformed to the laws of the state in which they were produced, to alter them to suit the changing requirements of different localities becomes fatal in many cases to their artistic beauty and symmetry, and ruinous to the manager whose skill, labor, and financial investment they represent.

In New York, where more children employed in the theatre are to be found than in any other city, the question of their schooling is claiming attention, and definite progress in providing it is being made. The Professional Children's School, which is allied with the Rehearsal Club—a self-sustaining institution organized by the late Rt. Rev. David H. Greer, D.D., and under the patronage of such responsible people as the Rev. Ernest M. Stires, D.D., William M. Embree, George H. Hedges, Dr. William S. Thomas, and Mrs. Richard Mansfield (forming the advisory board for 1918)—offers facilities throughout the school year for the instruction of child actors in general studies and exists under the sanction and authority of the New York Board of Education. None but children who work in the theatre are eligible to its classes. Its pupils are subject to the city's truant laws, and they may be transferred back or forth to corresponding grades in the public schools.

Its curriculum is the same that is followed in the regular schools, except that the hours for study and recitations are adapted to the special needs of the children who attend it. Even when its pupils are absent on long theatrical tours, facilities which enable them to continue their studies are afforded. It also offers annually three scholarships by which apt pupils may continue their education in excellent preparatory academies. So the claim can no longer be made that children employed in the theatre are denied educational advantages which are accessible to other children of their ages and circumstances.

There are always a considerable number of talented and more or less experienced child actors available to the theatrical manager. This is especially true in New York, where nearly all the important dramatic and musical productions of our native stage are made and have their initial runs. Some stage directors prefer to employ them because, within limitations, they are accustomed to stage surroundings and know about what is expected of them. As they have been more or less regularly before the public, a manager who is intending to produce a play which requires the use of children is able to observe their acting in other plays and decide whether they are suitable to his purposes.

But for my own productions which may happen to contain child characters I never depend upon these so-called professional children. I much prefer children in my casts who have had very little or no previous experience on the stage. As in the cases of my grown actors, I am always careful that they fit in appearance, and, as far as possible, in temperament also, the characters which they are to represent.

As I plan my productions far ahead, I am ever on the lookout for the right type of children, and I usually find them in the humble levels of city life. I train them according to my own methods and I can quickly discover whether they will be able to understand what they are expected to do. It does not need a child born in luxury to impersonate a well-to-do child character in a play. All little children, even the waifs in the gutter, think in the language and symbols of fairyland. As there is nothing more interesting than child psychology, so there is nothing more beautiful than a child's imagination, and it is upon these that I try to work.

In this way I avoid what to me is the most exasperating thing in the theatre—the child who is conscious of its own precocity. The great trouble with children who appear with any considerable degree of regularity on the stage is that they have been pampered and overcoached until they have lost all their naturalness. They have not been made to comprehend what they do, but go through certain actions and speak certain lines merely because they have been told to. The result is that they fall into the habit of moving about like little automatons, and this fatal fault, once having been acquired, can never be broken. It is due largely to the fact that they have been too much under the influence of a "stage mother" or of a director who is content to be only a coach. They become superficial and artificial, and the puppet strings are always visible in their acting.

These are some of the reasons why I always advise earnestly against putting a child on the stage at an early age, even when it has shown great precocity for acting or when it is the ambition of its parents to have it choose the theatre as a life profession. Many children recite well or develop early ability for memorizing and acting, and the natural pride of their mothers and fathers straightway puts the stage in their minds. If children have great natural talent, it should be left alone. When it is subjected to too much coaching, it disappears and generally it does not return.

Furthermore, the fact that a child acts well

on the stage gives no reason for belief that it will act equally well when it grows up. Even if it have the advantage of the most skilful training, there comes a time when it loses the pretty manner that, as a child, made it so interesting and attractive. The treble of its little voice, so delightful to the ear, begins to change to uncertain notes. It becomes awkward in the use of its hands and feet. It begins to be self-conscious and constrained in its movements. It outgrows the child characters it has played, just as it outgrows its costumes and the sentiments which the characters are introduced to express. For a time nothing is left for it to put in the place of these things. It is now in the transition state between childhood and young maturity which inevitably must come to every child. If this child had been kept out of the theatre altogether, if it had been prevented from accumulating the ingrained mannerisms and artificial ways that are common to almost all stage children, it would have had a much better chance of becoming a good actor in later life.

I have come across a good many children during my thirty-five years in the theatre who have afterward developed into actors of high attainments, but they have been the exceptions to the rule. I have also had, at times, very precocious children in my various companies. Little Percy Helton, who acted the child character of Willem in my own play, "The Return of Peter Grimm," was, for instance, a child of remarkable mental capacity and adaptability, and a little actor of amazing skill and appeal. But I have never exploited a child solely on account of its precocity. When I have presented children on my stages —which I have frequently done and shall continue to do—it has been because of the requirements forced upon me by the plays in which they have appeared, and not because of the children themselves.

A discussion of the problem of the child actor must not fail to take into account the case of Master Betty, the most remarkable example of juvenile precocity the English-speaking theatre—in fact, the theatre of the whole world in all time—has ever known.

This amazing prodigy, whose meteoric career came in the first years of the last century, was born in 1791, in Belfast, Ireland, of parents who were not connected with the theatre. His mental attainments seem to have been inherited from his mother. Before he was able to read he had learned to recite and could memorize long speeches from Shakespeare's plays, which he delivered with a keen sense of character and accompanied with appropriate action. As he grew older his remarkable gift was trained until, fearing that he might be led to choose a theatrical career, his parents began to discourage his love for acting, and he was sent away to school.

When Master Betty was eleven years old the great Mrs. Siddons paid a professional visit to Belfast, and the boy, temporarily home from school, was taken to see her in the part of Elvira in "Pizarro." Instantly his infatuation for acting flamed up again. After a sleepless night he stole out of the house, bought a copy of "Pizarro," and committed all of Elvira's speeches to memory before night.

Fearing that further interference with his passionate desire to act would injure his health, Master Betty's father took him to a Belfast theatrical manager, who heard him recite, and, declaring that he was an infant Garrick, offered him half the receipts of the house if he would appear in the Belfast Theatre. So it came about that he made his first public stage appearance, acting in the tragedy "Zara," in 1803, at the age of twelve.

The boy's genius electrified his audience and Dublin soon insisted upon seeing him. Here he was publicly lauded and privately fêted, and then Cork demanded a chance to worship him. By this time he was acting in farce as well as in tragedy and gradually accumulating a *répertoire* of plays.

Next he invaded Scotland. At Glasgow and Edinburgh, where his fame had preceded him, the theatres were not large enough to hold the clamoring crowds. London began to hear of the infant Rocius who was amazing the provinces, and Drury Lane Theatre and Covent Garden competed to secure him. The terms they offered were the largest that had ever been paid to an actor. John Philip Kemble was then receiving only the equivalent of $200 a week, yet the proprietors of Covent Garden were willing to pay Master Betty more than that sum for a single night.

The upshot was that Covent Garden and Drury Lane agreed to share his services and Master Betty appeared at the former theatre in 1804, at the age of thirteen, as Achmet in "Barbarossa." The chronicles of the times tell how the audience began to assemble as early as ten o'clock in the morning, and jammed the theatre by four in the afternoon. The Prince of Wales, afterward George IV, was in attendance, and the boxes were filled with the social and artistic élite of the town. After six nights of delirious adulation, the prodigy transferred to the Drury Lane Theatre, where the public burst down the doors and balustrades to get in. Royalty fêted him and the wealthy bestowed presents upon him which mounted into fortunes. Gentleman Smith, the original Charles Surface in "The School for Scandal," who had retired from the stage sixteen years before, gave the boy a seal cut in the likeness of David Garrick, which the great tragedian had presented to him with an injunction not to give it away until an actor had risen who was worthy of the gift.

This frenzy of the London public continued two years. It reached its climax when Pitt adjourned the House of Commons in order that its members might witness Master Betty in a performance of "Hamlet." Then the furor over the boy actor began to subside. By 1807 interest in Master Betty had declined, and the people, with their returning sense, for the first time suspected that the critics, whom they had driven from the town for questioning the depth and fiber of the prodigy's powers, had probably been right.

In 1808 little was heard of the marvel, and finally he entered Cambridge University, afterward becoming an inconspicuous captain in the North Shropshire Yeomanry Cavalry. As a boy, Master Betty could learn the entire rôle of "Hamlet" in four days; as a man, he had not a particle of his infantile theatrical genius left.

The descent of the youthful prodigies of our American stage has not been as precipitous as Master Betty's, because they have not soared to such exalted heights. But every father and mother whose young hopeful has distinguished itself as an actor in childhood should bear in mind the fate of this young Belfast phenomenon of the last century before planning a brilliant career in the theatre for it.

It is said of Master Betty that, in appearance, he was slight and feminine, with clearcut features, intelligent expression, and small eyes. His voice was rather monotonous and shrill in its higher notes. But before an audience he lost all consciousness of their presence in the identity of his representations. Let his peculiar genius be analyzed carefully and it will be found that he was a master of words, but not of ideas. No doubt he could play prettily. But once the allurement of childhood had disappeared, he found it a very different thing to act with the mastery of great art. Here lies always the stumbling-block in the pathway of the child actor.

III

There was a time in our native theatre when a number of avenues leading to careers in the theatre for children were open, but which no longer exist. One of the most direct of these was the epidemic of child "Pinafore" companies which spread over the country in the early 'eighties. The great success of the Gilbert and Sullivan operetta, both in London and in New York, suggested to some ingenious manager the idea of presenting it with children in the rôles, and for a number of years such amateur organizations were to be found everywhere.

THE PROBLEM OF THE CHILD ACTOR

A considerable number of our present actors received their first ideas of the stage and gained their elementary experience in this way. Julia Marlowe's genius might not have been detected if R. E. J. Miles, in Cincinnati, in 1879, had not cast for the rôle of Sir Joseph Porter the little girl of twelve who was then known as Sarah Frost. But, in her case, as I have stated before, it was long training outside the theatre that developed the great ability she afterward displayed. In the same year Mrs. Fiske, as little Minnie Maddern, was developing talent which has since become so conspicuous, as one of the numerous Ralph Rackstraws. Fritz Williams sang Sir Joseph Porter at fourteen; at the same age Annie Russell was one of the sisterhood of diminutive Josephines. Fay Templeton sang Ralph Rackstraw in 1880, and Annie Sutherland about this time appeared as Little Buttercup among the children who gave a season of "Pinafore" at Haverly's Chicago Theatre. William Collier, at eleven, was singing in the same operetta. Others whose first appearance in public came about in this way are Grace Filkins, Harry Woodruff, and Edna May—the last, of course, at a much later date.

Managers who did not know how, or, at least, did not care, to drill children for stage rôles found in these "Pinafore" companies a great reservoir on which they could draw at any time. Child players were more needed then than now, perhaps, for it was the period in which intense emotional acting was popular, and eminent stars who were in the ascendant were in the habit of securing their most poignant effects with the aid of children in the scenes.

The child actor was necessary to Clara Morris, as her performances in "Miss Multon" and many other emotional dramas in which she appeared reveal. The same applies to Madame Janauschek. Joseph Jefferson, J. K. Emmett, and, in later years, James A. Herne are other actors who were always at their best with little children as foils.

There are also three plays which have left an imprint on the native theatre, all of which were conspicuous for the number of children who at various times have appeared in them. A census of the child actors who have impersonated Little Eva in "Uncle Tom's Cabin" and the little folk in "Little Lord Fauntleroy" and "Editha's Burglar"—with which Elsie Leslie's name is best associated—would form a legion.

Some of the most interesting experiences I have ever had in the theatre have come out of the training of children for my productions, and the process of their training has involved much of the most important and perplexing work I have done. To teach a child to act in the stereotyped manner of most stage children is not very difficult; but to drill a child actually to impersonate character is a very different matter, which requires special faculties, not the least of which are infinite patience and great persistence.

When I am about to produce a play requiring children I have several of the right ages and types brought before me. I am careful to inquire, first of all, as to the motive of the parents in offering their children for employment. If I find among them a "stage mother" who has deluded herself into believing her child is a genius who will decide the fate of any play in which it appears, that child is very certain not to be engaged by me. I explain to a mother that I shall expect her to give the child every possible attention when it is not actually on the stage, but that every detail of its drill must be left to me.

Having found the right children for my purposes, the next important step is to become acquainted with them. It is fatal to the success of a child in the theatre if the stage director first approach it as a master. When the child is inclined to fear its teacher, or becomes constrained and embarrassed in his presence, it will never learn to act with freedom or naturalness.

So I sometimes spend hours in the process of getting acquainted. In my theatre in New

York there is a large rehearsal-room which can be turned into an excellent playroom, and I have it fixed up with toys so that it will be likely to attract a child's interest. During the rehearsals of my production of "Daddies," in which there were five little children who represented unfortunates that had been orphaned by the war, this room became much more a nursery than a rehearsal-room.

For a time I romp with the children, without mentioning the work they are about to do. This time—it may be several hours, or even days—I do not consider wasted. I am now getting the children to know me and to feel confidence in me. At the same time I am carefully observing them, studying their temperaments and natures and manners, and deciding what is the best way to mold them to my needs. We often have luncheon and dinner together, talk about everything that appeals to a child's fancy, and thus gradually get on familiar terms. Meanwhile my costume designers are also observing them to determine what will be most appropriate for them. It sometimes happens during this preliminary period of getting acquainted that I detect faults in a child which I feel I cannot overcome. Some children are superlatively imaginative and nervous; others are superlatively dull and phlegmatic. It is with these two extremes that it is hardest to deal.

At length I have decided as to the adaptability of the child, or children, and then I begin to lead them by degrees into the play in which they are to act. Some stage directors make the great mistake of teaching children only the lines which they are expected to speak and describing to them only the scenes in which they are to appear. That has never been my method. Instead, I am careful to explain the whole play to them. I try to make it appeal to their imaginations as a story. I want them to feel that every detail in it is personal to them. As there is no limit to a bright child's imagination, this is not such a difficult task as it seems—not even in the case of a very intricate drama. A little child can soon be taught to imagine that it has a father who is in prison, a mother who is ill and in need, or even that it is some one different than it really is.

When they have fully grasped the story and its meaning, I begin to teach them to go through their parts, either in the rehearsal-room or on the stage. Meanwhile they have been learning, invariably with great rapidity, the lines which they are to speak. I try to make them understand that they must do as I direct, and I caution the grown actors not to show the first sign of impatience if the little ones do not at first grasp what they are to do. When children are being drilled on my stage, I reserve for myself the sole right to be impatient or severe, and I make it a point never to exercise it.

I go over sentence after sentence with these little actors, showing them how to combine their movements with what they are saying. Generally I act out their rôles in detail for them, but I am particularly careful to warn them never to mimic me. My purpose is to impress upon them just what is to be done, and then induce them to do it in their own way. I find that unconsciously they absorb my meaning and quickly fit themselves into the complications of the play. How quickly this can be accomplished depends not so much upon how exact is the child's knowledge of what it is expected to do, but how clearly it comprehends what is the meaning of everything that is happening around it.

All children, of course, cannot be trained alike; in this respect they are not different from experienced adult actors. With some I get my best results by cooing and caressing, and with others by directing and coaxing. Like grown actors, also, I find that some child performers are able to speak their lines most effectively while sitting and that others can best carry out my intention while standing or moving about. In such matters as these it is the temperament of the child that decides.

When it comes time for a public performance, the children on my stage are the source of the slightest of my worries. By that time we are on a plane of companionship. I know exactly what they will do. I never fear that they will forget their lines. A bit of stage business may now and then escape their memories, but the lines of their parts they are sure to remember. In fact, it generally happens, by the time the preliminary rehearsals of a play are at an end, that the child actors in its cast have not only memorized perfectly all their own dialogue, but also that of all the other actors who appear in the scenes with them. Our audiences are very little aware how often a child actor saves the effect of an entire scene by prompting one of the older actors whose lines, through nervousness or inadvertence, have suddenly left him.

The child always takes its acting seriously. It seldom suffers from fear or embarrassment in an audience's presence. All that it has to do in a play becomes very real to it, and it loses consciousness of everything that lies beyond the footlights. How naturally it accomplishes its part depends on how free it is from the conventional manners which it may have acquired in other plays, and how careful has been the drill which it has undergone for its immediate work.

To all who may harbor a belief that the child actor is a poor little bond-slave, placed in the theatre before its time to earn its living, I would say that invariably it loves its work and its lot. In the great majority of cases it is an unfortunate child—compared with well-to-do children in normal domestic circumstances whose only thought is to breathe and eat and grow up. If the fortunes of all our lives were distributed more equally and justly—especially among our little folk—I would deplore a condition that makes it necessary for any child to earn a living for itself or for others.

But the conditions which affect people are not the same. Some children are destined to luxury and comfort, and some to want, even to neglect. I can only add that, if a child must work—no child really should have to work at all—the employment it finds in the theatre is more pleasant and less likely to do it physical harm than any other that is accessible to it.

The problem of the child actor is one which invites our wisest consideration. That it is a problem, we who are in the theatre know only too well. Yet the harshness of the problem is softened when we stop to consider for a moment the attitude of the child actor toward its work. It is work of which a child never wearies, work which to it means only play. Does any theatre-goer imagine that his own enjoyment of Barrie's "Peter Pan" was greater than that of the child actors who capered in its fanciful scenes?

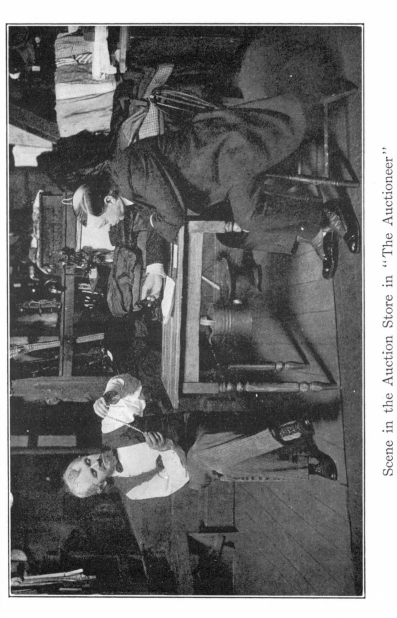

Scene in the Auction Store in "The Auctioneer"

Showing David Warfield as Simon Levi and Harry Lewellyn as Isaac Leavitt

The Electric Switchboard of the Belasco Theatre, the Largest
in America

Chapter V

IMPORTANT AIDS TO THE ACTOR'S ART

I

IN the experience of every one who chooses the fine arts as the field of his work, and succeeds to a reasonable degree in accomplishing the results which he has set as the goal of his ambition, there must come a time when he can look back with satisfaction upon hostile criticism. My own endeavor has always been devoted to the art of the theatre. As it is the most democratic of all the arts, and is therefore subject constantly to scrutiny and study from the most divergent points of view, I have not escaped the inevitable penalty of being sometimes misunderstood.

In one branch of the art of the theatre, especially, my purposes and methods have aroused discussion which has resulted in extremes of encouraging approval or discouraging objection. There was a time when it was charged against me that I placed undue emphasis upon stage decoration, the use of light and color, of scenic investiture and minute detail of costuming; that I held the importance of these adjuncts above the play itself and its interpretation through the acting art.

It was argued by those who disparaged my methods, or mistook my purposes, that the chief effort in my dramatic productions was to appeal to the eye and to subordinate the work of the dramatist, which must be the foundation of every production of the stage, to mere external display. This view of my work as a dramatic producer, which was sometimes expressed twenty-five years ago, but has undergone a radical and significant change as time has advanced, caused me to be regarded in some quarters as a kind of stage carpenter or decorator who was attempting to veil some sort of hocus-pocus by the pretense of art.

At the same time, my method of presenting plays was never without its strong advocates. The latter saw more clearly than my adverse critics. They divined that the careful attention I gave to the extraneous details of my productions was only for the purpose of intensifying and interpreting the mood of the play and of the characters, and that I was trying by legitimate artistic means to stir the emotions of my audiences.

In some of these controversies I have been hailed as a wizard of color and light and in other equally superlative terms. For such encouraging support I have always been grateful, but for the final verdict I have looked with confidence to the best taste of the public. A worker in the arts is never on unsafe ground when he courts both praise and blame; he is in danger only when he is ignored.

It was my fortune to come into the theatre during a time when lighting appliances and the use of illuminating effects were undergoing a great scientific revolution. The invention and perfection of the electric light fall easily within this period. It is usual to consider the inventions of Thomas A. Edison from the viewpoint of their scientific, commercial, and practical utility. We of the theatre realize how great also is the debt which the dramatic producer's art owes for its present perfection to this magician who is not of the theatre and into whose calculations the benefits which the stage was to derive from his discoveries probably did not at first enter.

My first work as a producer of plays was done in the Far West, where the theatre was still in a primitive state. I was, of course, much hampered by the imperfect methods of illumination which were then at our command. I began with flickering candles and smelly oil-lamps, and observed the improvement when they, in turn, were replaced by gas.

Each of these changes brought me a step nearer to the ideals which I had formed in my dreams, but which then still seemed far away. It was inevitable that I should utilize to the fullest extent every new means by which the true effects of nature could be more closely reproduced in the theatre. So it is upon applying to the stage's art electric lighting, and the more perfect use of color which it has made possible, that a great part of my thought and energies as a dramatic producer has been concentrated.

By good fortune my work in the New York theatre, with its wider facilities, began about the time of the transition from the stock-company system of presenting plays to productions which were made with a view to greater permanence, in which more careful attention could be given to the details of their staging. This change in the management of theatres offered better opportunity and at the same time greater incentive for experiment with delicate illuminating effects.

Before that time it had been the practice, as a means of stirring the feelings of audiences or intensifying the emotional effect of a speech or situation, to have some sort of a musical interpretation accompany the play. A trace of the custom still survives in the term "melo-drama," which implies drama with a musical accompaniment; but my conviction was that the most powerful emotional appeal could be made and the strongest interpretative power gained by the use of color and light.

IMPORTANT AIDS TO THE ACTOR'S ART

From the time when, as a boy, I used to play with toy theatres lighted with lamps, I have tried to reach my audiences through their sensitiveness to color and light. Later, when I became stage director for managers who did not have the financial resources to provide even adequate scenic decoration, I made my strongest appeal in the same way. To use color, not for mere adornment, but to convey a message to the hearts of audiences, has become my creed. The proof that I am right is my love of nature and my intuitive knowledge of its moods.

I recall that when I was a child I delighted in watching the changing effects of light upon the mountains, the ravines, the river-banks, and the sea. Every hue in the heavens by day or by night interested me; and then I began to study the moods of nature.

For nature is as complex in her moods as a woman. Mark the lowering anger of a March day, with its driving clouds and frowning, barren landscape. But April is all tears and smiles, symbolizing the spirit of awakening nature and growing things. Let one watch the changing hues of the grasses and leaves on a midsummer afternoon to understand how restless and variable are nature's moods. October, with its russets and browns, suggests the mood of sadness; and winter, spreading its coverlet of white, breathes peace and rest.

One needs only read the inexhaustible book of nature to learn and feel all these moods.

In the same way colors bear a direct relation to the moods and traits of human nature. It has been no mere convention or habit in their use which has established this fact. There is something instinctively regal in the purple, so it has become the symbol of kings. White stands for youth and innocence and purity. Red typifies the tragedy of life, with its accompaniment of hideousness and violence. Look upon the drab and the gray, and instinctively you become sedate and grave. Black stands for somber things—the accepted symbol of mourning and death.

Romantic impulse springs from the half-lights, and thus the twilight, with its silvery blue, is the hour for lovers' trysts. Observe the effect of the yellow gleam of a lamp, shining from a window into the darkness, and note the feeling of half-fear that involuntarily steals over you. Yet courage comes in the clear white light of the noonday sun. Look upon the sickly moon and detect at once a feeling of sadness. Our greatest novelists have never failed to take advantage of these psychological phenomena of color upon the imagination to intensify the spell into which they cast the reader.

If, as I conceive it, the purpose of the theatre be to hold the mirror up to nature, I know of no better place to obtain the effects of nature than to go to nature itself. To fulfil this purpose with integrity, to surround the mimic life of the characters in drama with the natural aspects of life, to seek in light and color the same interpretative relation to spoken dialogue that music bears to the words of a song, is, I contend, the real art, the true art of the theatre. He who goes direct to nature for the effects he introduces on the stage can never be wrong, because nature itself is never wrong. It is upon this creed that I base my faith in realism in dramatic art.

The trouble is, however, that a school of decorators has grown up within the theatre which is trying to improve upon the effects of nature. Thus has risen the so-called "new art" of the stage. It has resulted in the eccentricities of coloring and lighting that in very recent years have been having a fitful vogue. My own belief is that it is not only a negation of truth, but a waste of time, to try to improve upon nature, because from it emerges the tawdry, the bizarre, and the unreal.

This movement has not been confined wholly to the theatre, but has spread among all the other fine arts. It has been utilized by unskilled workers in the arts to conceal their deficiencies, and it has been lauded and championed by faddists who are always ready to fancy that they discern sublime truth in things that to normal eyes are grotesque and unreal. It has manifested itself in the theatre in opaque backings, in the vivid, deadly colorings of extreme impressionism, and in exaggerated architecture.

Yet out of all this eccentricity—this striving to be "different" at any cost—much good is eventually to come. Already this effort to exaggerate the effects of nature is providing its own antidote. From it all will re-emerge the real art of the theatre, which will be found to constitute just this—lighting, coloring, simplicity, according to the established laws of nature.

It must be borne in mind in this connection that methods and fashions on the stage are variable and that the theatre always reflects the taste and proclivities of its own time. As the day of the cluttered and overcrowded drawing-room is past, so is the time of the overdecorated stage. It is not necessary to look to the theatre to find the evidence of this radical change in taste. Every interior decorator who is commissioned to furnish a home and make it livable shapes his work in accordance with the new tendency. He now hangs few pictures or ornaments on the walls. The furniture he provides is only such as is required for actual and practical use. Simplicity has become the key-note of every tasteful home, and the same tendency toward simplicity extends even to the making and arrangement of a flower-garden.

If the stage director of a modern play of only a few years ago had limited his decorative scheme to the simplicity for which he now strives, his work would surely have been subject to general protest. Those were the years when homes were pretentiously ornate, and audiences consequently demanded similar effects in the mimic homes of the stage. It was then that the large expense involved in the scenic mounting of a drama was accepted as the measure of its appropriateness and effectiveness.

But who can tell how long this present taste for simplicity will prevail? Fashions change constantly among the people, and their influence upon the decorative art of the theatre is immediate. I am not so sure that the now prevailing taste will continue long, for what suits the present hour never appeals strongly to the next.

Acting and all kinds of stage "business" also change with the times, in order to keep in harmony with their surroundings. The actor's method is now keyed to the note of naturalism. The excessive restlessness on the stage which prevailed a decade or so ago has given way to restfulness. The deportment of characters in a play is now the same as the deportment of well-mannered people in the privacy of their homes. There is less sitting on tables, less crossing and recrossing the stage at regular intervals, less squatting on sofas, and less bouncing from chair to chair. The stage decorator shows himself to be most resourceful and efficient, and helps best to aid the art of the theatre when he succeeds in preserving the tension and interest of a scene while his characters hardly move from their positions.

Whether the scene be an exterior or interior, no matter what be the subject with which it is concerned, one of the great assisting factors in strengthening its appeal to an audience is the stage decorator's skilful use and manipulation of lights. Indeed, the regulation and diffusion of light, and the arrangement of color effect in a simply furnished sitting-room scene, are not less important, and also not much less difficult, than the creation of what may seem to be a far more intricately contrived sunset panorama.

Because I have preferred to move cautiously, and have not been influenced by every new eccentricity of stage-lighting, I will not plead guilty to being unprogressive in this important department of dramatic production. Of late there has been a good deal of discussion concerning the more natural effects to be gained by the omission of footlights, which almost invariably cast unnatural shadows upon the scenery and the faces of the actors. To do away with footlights has even been heralded as a new and important innovation in the art of the stage director.

But it happens that as far back as my production of "The Passion Play" in San Francisco, thirty-five years ago, I presented whole scenes without resorting to footlights, and I used the now antiquated but recently revived "bull's-eyes" set along the balcony railing to obtain the effect of level rays. In the days of the old Madison Square Theatre I omitted footlights in the presentation of "The Rajah" and in some of the scenes in the elder De Mille's "Delmore's Daughters"—plays now almost forgotten—and for the most impressive effects I secured in "The Darling of the Gods" of fifteen years ago, in such scenes as the Bamboo Forest, the River of Souls, and the Death Chamber, footlights were entirely discarded. In "Adrea" not a footlight was turned on during the play, and the same course was followed in "The Return of Peter Grimm," "The Phantom Rival," and "Marie-Odile," when certain scenes in these plays justified it.

I did not call attention to these changes from the usual method of lighting a stage, and I never regarded them as innovations or discoveries; to me they were only a means to an end—a natural and consistent way of accomplishing certain effects which I thought necessary for the proper production of these particular plays.

II

In our American playhouses it is not usual to find a workshop fully equipped with machinery and provided with power necessary for running it. But for years, ever since I was financially able to maintain it, I have had an experimental electrical laboratory in the basement of my theatre. So far as I am aware, it is the only one of its kind in the world. Every illuminating appliance I have ever used on my stages has been invented in it. At any hour in the day, and often far into the night, experts are busy with me or under my direction in this unique little workshop, experimenting with my light and color devices, trying by every means that ingenuity can suggest to bring my stage into closer harmony with the secrets of nature. Even Mr. Edison in his great laboratories is not more industrious than we.

Many of the inventions we have developed here have been adopted in theatres all over the world. Very often theatrical experts have come from Europe to study our methods, and it has been a common thing for workmen to obtain jobs on my mechanical staff only for the purpose of discovering all they can and then carrying their knowledge back to the

The "Light Bridge" of the Belasco Theatre

This bridge is placed horizontally above the proscenium arch and from it are operated "baby lights" (miniature spot lights) which work in conjunction with the battery of perpendicular baby lights on each side of the proscenium arch

Machine-shops in the Second Sub-cellar Under the Belasco Theatre

This is the only playhouse in New York that has a machine-shop operated by power. Here are made all the new lighting and mechanical effects used in David Belasco's dramatic productions

The Shops Where Mr. Belasco's Lighting Apparatus Is Manufactured and Experiments in Stage-lighting Are Constantly Being Carried On

The Belasco is the only theatre in New York that contains a completely equipped machine-shop

producers who sent them to my shop. But such secret tactics are unnecessary. Every one is invited to come in and watch us if he wishes, because whatever devices I use in one production will be changed and improved in the next. We try never to stand still; our motto is always to keep moving ahead.

It happens that time and money are often wasted in our underground workshop, from which other theatrical managers get the benefit. I have spent as much as $5,000 in an effort to imitate certain delicate colorings of a sunset, and have ended by throwing aside the scene altogether. When I was preparing "The Girl of the Golden West" I experimented an entire summer to reproduce the hazy, shifting hues of the sun as it sinks below the Sierra Nevada Mountains in California. It was a very beautiful sunset that we contrived, but it was not even remotely Californian. So we proceeded to something else and I sold that sunset scene, which had been the fruits of three months' work, to another manager for a nominal sum and he afterward used it with great success in one of his own productions.

In the same way many other effects which cost me thousands of dollars to accomplish, owing to the amount of experimenting they required, have been copied by others at trivial cost.

In my workshop was invented the new system of horizontal lighting which made necessary the complete architectural remodeling of the stage of the Belasco Theatre before the production of "The Boomerang" in the autumn of 1915. Within a year every theatre in New York which makes any effort at progressiveness had adopted the hood and side-lights, with their peculiar dimmers and reflectors which formed the basis of the process.

Years before this the "Du Barry lights" and "baby lights," which afterward went all over the world, had their origin in my laboratory. It may be of interest to know that the former, which I invented for my production of "Du Barry," were brought into existence on account of the brilliant red of Mrs. Leslie Carter's hair and the peculiar coloring of her complexion.

She was like an April day—all sunshine and rain—and, as she was a woman of great passion and power, her emotional scenes would tend to accentuate the lines in her face and take away her beauty. I saw at once that the lights which were suitable for the other actors in the company, both in hue and intensity, were not adapted to her. They might make the other actresses beautiful, but they made Mrs. Carter look hideous. To counteract this effect I contrived a system of small, moving individual lights which were kept fixed upon the important characters as they moved about the stage.

On account of Mrs. Carter's coloring, the light constantly cast upon her was a delicate pink which tended to accentuate her beauty by softening the sheen of her hair and removing the lines from her face. The device was simple enough—after some one had first thought of it —and ever afterward it has been a blessing to red-haired actresses. I suspect, too, that a good many matrons have taken advantage of it in arranging the decorations of their private drawing-rooms.

Any dramatic producer who works for the best artistic effects in the theatre must have an intuitive knowledge of color, and he must also know his geography well. The caprices of nature have always had an intense fascination for me. Nature, in each far-separated locality of the earth, has given a different appearance to the sun and moon and stars and sky, and to the vegetation and fruit and snow and sea. Nature has also given to the peoples of these differing localities their own peculiar esthetic sense of color. If any one doubts that the Japanese have a different sense of the values and relationships of colors from our own, let him study their kimonos or their potteries or their landscape paintings.

I am convinced that the esthetic satisfaction which the public found in my production of "The Darling of the Gods" was due as much to its effects of color, light, and costumes as to its story and acting. Every particle of color used on the stage, every ray of light cast upon its scenes, was carefully calculated to symbolize its moods, interpret its meaning, and direct and strengthen its emotional appeal. I meant that its lighting accompaniment should stand in the same relation to it as music written by a composer to express and elaborate the thought and sentiment of a poem.

I foresaw that it would be hard for my audiences to step out of the glare and excitement of the New York streets and enter at once into the mood and spirit of ancient Japan. To put them in a receptive state I began the story of the revolt of the outlawed Samurai and their betrayal by the Princess Yo-San, to save the life of their leader, Prince Kara, her lover, by showing a series of tableaux symbolical of the theme of the play. I called this silent picture "The Chase and Death of the Butterfly," and made it indicate what was to be the fate of the heroine. It was timed to picture Japan in the spring, when the cherry blossoms are in half-bloom, and it showed the lapse of the hours from the bright sunshine of midday to the gloom of night—suggestive of the passing of a life.

It led to an interior scene which I called "The Feast of a Thousand Welcomes," brilliantly illuminated by varicolored lanterns, for now I was suggesting to my audiences the ceremonials and festivities of Japanese life. To increase the delicacy of the effect I inclosed the stage in silk draperies, for the Japanese, more than any people, are sensitive to soft colors.

Each chapter of the story was enveloped in lights to fit its moods. So I passed to the *shoji*, or paper house, of Yo-San, bathed in moonlight and close to a running brook, to be indicative of the romance of the unsuspecting lovers as the spies of Zakkuri, the Minister of War, lay in wait for Kara to arrest him as a traitor.

Thus the play proceeded to the ancient sword-room of the relentless Zakkuri, who now had made Kara his captive, and was endeavoring to force Yo-San to betray the hiding-place of the Samurai as the price for saving him from torture. This picture of the War Minister's palace was vaulted, high-pillared, gloomy, and sinister, to suggest the cruel nature of the man. At intervals the doors leading to the dungeons below were opened, lighting the scene with the red glow of the torture-chamber to which Kara was soon to be sent.

The suspense and thrill of this scene were gained solely by my manipulation of lights. I might have played it in its entirety in pantomime and made it express just as much. In the torture scene in Victorien Sardou's "La

Tosca" a sense of horror was communicated by the sound of the agonized cries of the suffering Marie; but my scene was all silence, and I worked upon the imaginations of my audiences by the sinister glare of the torture-fires as Zakkuri craftily wrung from Yo-San the confession which meant life to Kara, but death to his faithful band.

Eventually came the scene of the red bamboo forest where the surrounded Samurai, with Yo-San, their betrayer, and Kara, her lover, commit honorable suicide by hara-kiri. Behind the gaunt trees I showed a great, blood-red descending moon, symbolical of ebbing life. I shrouded this picture in deep shadows and painted it in the color tones of tragedy. My purpose was to veil from the audiences the actual incidents of the death of the Samurai, which might be repulsive, but to impress the full meaning of the tragedy upon their imaginations. When they had heard the clatter of the armor as the last man fell, the moon had sunk out of sight, leaving the stage in darkness and silence.

The tragedy of the play having been completed, it became necessary to represent the ascension of Yo-San to the celestial heavens to meet the waiting Kara, after her condemnation for her betrayal of the Samurai to ten thousand years in the Shinto purgatory. With the possible exception of certain scenes in

"The Return of Peter Grimm," it was the most audacious scene I have ever undertaken to represent on a stage. Literally, it meant that a very earthly Yo-San had to be shown rising skyward to meet a healthy Kara sitting on a cloud. If the picture became for a moment ridiculous, if it stirred so much as a ripple of laughter, the dignity of the entire play would be lost.

We began by painting the clouds and the heavens in colors, but I could see nothing but the paint. Each time Yo-San ascended she reminded me of nothing so much as Little Eva in "Uncle Tom's Cabin." It became very evident to me that colored scenery would not do; I found I would have to contrive the effect by shadows and illusions gained by lights.

So I surrounded Yo-San with white, unpainted canvas, and began experimenting to evolve a color suggestive of celestial blue—not the pale blue of the sky, but the radiant blue of the heavens above the sky, to which no audience could take valid exception, of course, because they had never been to heaven. I wanted only to excite their imagination and make them see in Yo-San the symbol of a liberated soul.

I secured the requisite shade of blue by throwing an intense white light through powerful lenses covered with peculiar blue silk. When these rays fell upon the white-canvas scenery they became partly absorbed and produced exactly the right indefinite, far-away effect. Over all was spread a gauze veil which tended to soften the scene. The figures of Yo-San and Kara were held in deep shadows, so deep that their outlines could barely be seen as they approached each other with arms outstretched.

Hundreds of experts came to study this final scene in "The Darling of the Gods," and all agreed that its ethereal and spiritual suggestion was perfect. But what would have been the amazement of an audience if the special lights had suddenly been cut off and the ordinary lights of the stage turned on! They would have discovered nothing more than Blanche Bates and Robert T. Haines dressed in white and surrounded with strips of unpainted cloth.

The artistic success and the popular appeal of "The Darling of the Gods" were sufficient to justify my faith in the use of color and light to communicate to audiences the underlying symbolism of a play. Yet it is only a part of the uses to which these important adjuncts to every dramatic production may be put. It is equally within the province of a stage director to employ the same agencies to produce the effects of realism.

When I produced "The Rose of the Rancho," the romantic drama which established Frances

Starr as a star, one of the problems that I had to solve was how to make the physical discomfort and mental lassitude caused by the noon heat of a midsummer day in southern California seem actual to a theatre audience. Every one who is familiar with the climate knows that at such a time the sun beats fiercely down upon the earth—that under its withering rays no man or beast can work.

Upon such a scene, representing a garden outside a mission church, it was necessary to lift the curtain of "The Rose of the Rancho." The impression that the audience would first gain was to establish the note of languor which was to be constant through the remainder of the play. To be successful I must impart to them the most vivid suggestion possible of stifling and enervating heat.

I experimented a long time without satisfactory results. I had been using intense white lights, but the effect they produced upon painted canvas was not what I desired. The glare was there, but not the suggestion of heat. Then it occurred to me to cover the lamps on my stage with yellow silk and change the adobe walls of the church to negligible colors which would absorb the rays. By this means I obtained exactly the effect of dry, hot sunlight. It seemed as if the sun were actually burning into the plaster walls.

Into this stage picture I brought a slumbering Spanish padre, a water-girl half asleep, and two drowsy donkeys and their driver, who was deep in slumber. For six minutes I was able to hold this scene without a sound or movement on the stage, except an occasional snore from the sleeping padre and a yawn or two from the stupefied donkey-driver. The audience looked and listened, and literally felt the heat of a tropical day. Many people told me the scene was so real that it became actually uncomfortable.

Scores of lighting experts came to study the process I used, and this silent scene from "The Rose of the Rancho," which preceded the first spoken dialogue, has since been imitated every-where in the theatre, and often with similarly realistic effect. To persons not familiar with the use of color on the stage it probably did not seem difficult to contrive; nevertheless, its realism was secured only after weeks of patient experiment and through the most delicate combinations of pigments and light.

Such effects as these, and dozens of others I might cite from a list of perhaps twoscore productions I have made in my theatres, are, of course, more noticeable to the layman when used in romantic and fantastic plays than in modern dramas, in which the scenes are laid in interiors and among the conventional sur-roundings of contemporaneous, every-day life. By the broader, more vivid stage pictures the eye is consciously assailed. But there are also thousands of chances for delicate strokes of illumination in a well-managed modern play which neither audience nor critic is likely to notice, yet which work unconsciously upon the feelings and imagination.

To select the right opportunities for their use, to know how to contrive them, and at the same time how to conceal them, is what makes the profession of the stage director so difficult. Not only should he have a comprehensive knowledge of all the arts, he must understand psychology and the physical sciences besides. In the intricate process of producing a play he must be the translator of its moods, and supply the medium by which they are transmitted to audiences.

III

In the production of any play the laymen who compose a theatre audience go on the assumption that the perfect interpretation of the work as it comes from the dramatist's pen depends upon the actors whose business is it to portray the distinguishing peculiarities of the characters and to speak the lines written for them, in accordance with the stage director's conception of their meaning. If this were all there is to the making of a dramatic production, the stage director's task would be comparatively simple. It is also his important business to read and interpret the invisible writing expressed in moods which lie between the lines of the play.

By subtle use of light, and without altering so much as a word of the dramatist's text, it is possible sometimes to change completely the impression which a whole scene conveys. Often upon such a change may depend the fate of the play itself. The success of Hermann Bahr's comedy, "The Concert," when I produced it in America, contrasted with its quick failure when subsequently it was acted in London, is an instance that shows the responsibility which rests upon the stage director. In its case the fortunes of the whole production depended upon the discreet handling of a single scene that did not require more than ten minutes to present.

This play, by a prominent Austrian dramatist, is the story of the infatuation of a weak, sentimental, and highly romantic young woman, the wife of a phlegmatic but indulgent husband, for her music-teacher. He is a volatile and temperamental genius of the piano, a creature of uncontrollable impulses, but ·his sensible and devoted wife thoroughly understands him. The adoration of his headstrong pupil leads her to arrange an elopement, and she runs away with him to his bungalow in the Catskills, with rosy visions of perfect bliss.

Although the play is a comedy, this scene in the bungalow, which forms the second act, is really a domestic tragedy. Into it presently enters the deserted husband and also the wife of the runaway musician. To cure them of their infatuation, these two pretend that they, too, have fallen in love and are content with the course of events.

As the scene was to end in reconciliation, it became necessary at any cost to preserve the audience's sympathy for the eloping wife. To accomplish this purpose I raised the curtain upon an afternoon scene, to suggest the idea of frivolity. In the full light of day the wife would be able to resist the caresses of her amorous music-teacher and to realize the indiscretion into which she had plunged herself. While the sun still shone, she was able to hold herself in check. But as the shadow lengthened and twilight fell, romantic impulse overcame her and her self-control relaxed. Now was approaching the danger hour. As the musician sat at the piano and strummed on the keys, the door gradually opened and she stealthily entered, showering flowers over him in the dim light and embracing him as he played. Such a scene could have been acted only in the twilight and under the romantic mood such an hour invoked. If it had been shown in the broad light of day, the situation would have been impossible for the woman and instinctively offensive to the audience.

With the unexpected arrival of the other pair I caused the caretaker of the bungalow to enter and turn up the lights. Then each of the four could distinctly see the faces of the others. The hour for explanations had come and the spell of romance was removed from the situation. The understanding wife of the musician meanwhile moved quietly around the room, arranging the supper and fixing the chair and pillows for his comfort. Then she proposed their customary game of checkers, and, as they played, the other woman sat at the window, neglected and forgotten, in the cold gray of the moonlight which suggested that she had passed out of his life.

The lighting treatment of this act in "The Concert" brought the note of genuine romance into the play and saved it from seeming to be tawdry and merely scandalous. When it was acted in London in the full light of day the act was regarded as vulgar, and the reconciliation with which it ended was judged to be inconsistent with what had gone before. The result was that there it ran only eight performances, while at my theatre in New York it continued through an entire season without at any time provoking criticism on the score of vulgar suggestiveness.

Those who have seen my more recent production of "The Boomerang" may not have realized how important to its second act is the handling of the lights in the sitting-room, not only to emphasize moods, but also to change at different moments the appearance of the scene, and thus control the attention of the audience. If these expedients escaped notice altogether, they were the more successful because it was my intention that their effect should be unconsciously felt.

It was one of the most perplexing scenes I have ever directed, for there were no very strong situations to work with, and the dialogue could not be relied upon alone to carry it along. Besides, it practically involved the introduction of a new plot. The story of the lovesick youth was temporarily thrust aside, in order to bring in the budding romance of the physician and nurse—the boomerang of the physician's formula of treating his patient which was to recoil upon himself.

How to hold the attention of the audience for twenty-five minutes while the characters merely sat and talked was the problem which I had to solve. By acting the scene with the lights up I found I could make scarcely any impression at all. Then I decided to vary the lights and have them enforce the moods of the characters. So the curtain was lifted upon a room dimly lit, save for a log burning in the fireplace and a lamp casting its rays upon a card-table where the nurse sat. She was trying to keep the boy's thoughts fixed upon the game to help him forget the girl with whom he was foolishly infatuated. On the distant side of the room, and under another lamp, the boy's mother sat at her sewing, her manner betraying always her solicitude for him. In this way I was able to make the scene indicate something that was not in the dialogue. It emphasized a mood. Pictorially it was good, and psychologically it was right, because it was the truth.

As the story progressed into the physician and nurse's romance, I found a pretext for changing the lights and varying the illumination on the faces of the characters. To examine her chart and show the boy some pictures, the nurse touched a button and turned on a chandelier, permitting what followed to be played under altered illumination, with a corresponding altered effect upon the audience. At last the stand-lamps in the room were put out altogether and the lights at the back were turned up, again varying the appearance of the scene and unconsciously introducing another mood. In this manner I kept the attention of the audience always in control while acquainting them with the undramatic details of the story which were needed for the play's later development. Had the scene been permitted to unfold without these changes and gradations of light to fit its moods, a vital though undramatic half-hour in the middle of "The Boomerang" would possibly have been disclosed to be somewhat monotonous, and the play might not have lasted, as it did, through more than a year's unbroken succession of performances at my theatre.

Any play worth producing at all is entitled to the most perfect interpretation that can be secured for it. Any means that aids the audience's grasp and understanding of it, or that appeals to the esthetic sense, is useful and legitimate in the theatre—provided the stage director never loses sight of the fact that, when all is said and done, the play itself is the main thing, that the actors are always the chief instruments through which the story is to be told, and that the scene is only a background against which the dramatist's work is being projected.

If for however brief a time scenery, accessories, or any of the details of the environment, no matter how clever they be in themselves, distract the audience's attention from the play proper or cease to be other than mere assisting agencies, their value is destroyed and they become more a hindrance than an aid and, consequently, an inartistic blunder. One must remember that in nature the glory and beauty of the stars are never obliterated by the background of the sky.

In arranging a production I permit the play
to establish the environment in which it is to
be set. Its theme—and this alone—must be
the basis for everything else that follows.
The color schemes must be chosen to agree
with it, in the same sense that the actors must
be selected with regard to their fitness for
the characters. As I would not begin the
actual work of mounting a play without first
having settled upon its cast, I also try to work
out every essential detail of scenery, light, and
costumes before I set about the practical work
of the production itself.

In selecting my actors I even take into consideration their complexion and the color of
their hair. If there are several girls or boys
in a family, I try to have the girls resemble
the mother and the boys look like the father.
Such seemingly trivial details as these are
not always detected by the theatregoer, but
the general effect of the play is, after all,
greatly aided by them. In arranging the
groupings on the stage I prefer, if possible,
not to place two pronounced brunettes together, or two pronounced blondes.

Most of all, I endeavor always to protect the
appearance of the women on my stage. The
men do not matter so much, but the women
should be given the benefit of every possible
lighting effect. For instance, I would not
throw on the features of a brunette the same

quality of light that I would put on a blonde. In working out the color and lighting details of every production the careful stage director must always keep in consideration their effect upon the star; he may believe that he is not influenced by them; but he is, nevertheless.

Ordinarily I decide upon all matters of costumes myself, although in regard to the leading women in my companies I take care, as far as possible, to defer to their personal tastes. In the end, the costumes must harmonize with the predominating color scheme of the stage. In order to keep in my own complete control this important detail of a dramatic production, I provide all the clothing worn by the people in my companies. It is the ordinary practice, in the case of fancy costumes, for the producer to supply them, but so-called modern clothing is expected to be furnished by the actors themselves. But I have found it advisable to regulate every detail which enters into productions on my stages, and the advantage I gain by such caution greatly outweighs the expense.

It is much easier to provide the wardrobe for a historical or costume play than for a drama of contemporaneous social life. In the former class of plays the costume designer can be guided by the descriptions of the modes of the period in which the story is laid, and he also has the works of famous painters to assist

him.   Moreover, in such productions the vivid
coloring of the costumes can more readily
be made a part of the general color scheme
of the scenes.   It is easy to see that, in plays
which are purely fantastic, the imagination
and artistic perceptions of the costume designer have their fullest sweep.

But in costuming a modern play many
difficulties arise, because it is necessary always
to give heed to the fashions of the passing
hour, which are whimsical and subject to constant change.   I always hold to one method.
First, after consultation with my actors and
scene-painters, I settle upon the general color
effects I intend to use.   Then I instruct my
actors and actresses to imagine themselves
to be in the stations in life which their characters represent, and to go for their wardrobe to such places as these persons would be
likely to go.   If they are to appear in a play
of polite social life, I send them to the best
Fifth Avenue modistes and tailors.   If, on
the other hand, they belong to a humbler
stratum in life, I instruct them to observe such
economy and tastes as these humbler people
would be likely to use.

For instance, all the costumes in "The
Boomerang" were bought in the smartest
up-town shops in New York, while the wardrobe used in "The Music Master"—all except
David Warfield's seedy frock-coat—came from

the ready-made and second-hand clothing-stores of the East Side. The old frock-coat which Mr. Warfield always has worn when he has appeared as Anton von Barwig was bought from a man who had worn it at his wedding twenty years before the production of the play. Mr. Warfield is wearing it still, notwithstanding that "The Music Master" was first acted fifteen years ago.

When I produced "The Darling of the Gods" I sent to Japan for the costumes of my principal actors, as well as for the other paraphernalia of its scenes. When I presented "Du Barry" I sent a commissioner to France, where he purchased the rich fabrics and had them dyed to reproduce exactly the dresses and styles of the Court of Louis XV, as shown by portraits painted during that period.

The problem of obtaining appropriate costumes, however, varies with every play. I have dumfounded a tramp by asking him to exchange the coat on his back for a new one. Sometimes a poor girl of the street has attracted my attention because she was like a character I had in mind. I have sent for her and bought her dress, hat, shoes, and stockings. My wardrobe people have rummaged for weeks through pawnshops and second-hand stores to find a vest or some other article of apparel appropriate to an eccentric character in one of my plays. From fashionable dressmakers and tailors have come bills that would stagger a rich society woman.

But all these adjuncts of lighting, color, and costumes, however useful they may be, and however pleasing to an audience, really mark the danger-point of a dramatic production. No other worker in the American theatre has given so much time and energy to perfecting them as I; nevertheless, I count them as valuable only when they are held subordinate to the play and the acting. The stage always accomplishes more through the ability of its actors than through the genius of its scenic artists and electrical experts. And if the theatre in this country now is in a state of decline, it is because too much attention is being paid to stage decoration, important as it is when held in its proper place, and too little to the work of the players.

It is at once significant and deplorable that our scenic artists study continually, our actors seldom. And it is a fact that, except in the rarest cases, the more indifferent the quality of the acting the more elaborate is likely to be the surroundings in which it is found. If the artistic success of a play depended principally upon its scenery and decorations, any one who could afford to engage a good painter might become a dramatic producer almost overnight. And if this be the end sought by dramatic art, then we have had no past theatre.

IMPORTANT AIDS TO THE ACTOR'S ART

Shakespeare would doubtless have utilized every accessory and aid known to our modern stage, yet the greatness of his dramatic genius was established without them.

Only when the stage director is resolved that the play shall stand first in importance in a theatre production can he safely employ the countless pictorial aids which contribute to its effect and its appeal. Only when he relies upon his actors as the chief means of its interpretation should he venture upon those other agencies which help to bring it into closer relation with life and nature.

In short, to paraphrase Hamlet's words, the play must always be the thing, whether to stir the esthetic impulse of the public or to catch the conscience of the king.

Chapter VI

THE DRAMA'S FLICKERING BOGY —
THE MOVIES

I

MOTION pictures have stirred a great amount of unreasonable antipathy among people who have chosen the spoken drama as the field of their artistic work, and much of it, I suspect, has been caused by two very human weaknesses—selfishness and fear.

Since the process of photographing objects in motion was discovered a little less than twenty-five years ago, and a way was found, shortly afterward, to exhibit them on a screen before large assemblages, an additional amusement has been brought into a world in which there is so much care, anxiety, and distress that it is entitled to all the relaxation it can get. If for no better reason than this, motion pictures have justified themselves, and any

---

NOTE.—The growth of the motion picture has been rapid and, consequently, the trend of its future development is difficult to foretell. Therefore these comments are restricted to what it has accomplished as a medium of popular entertainment up to 1919.—DAVID BELASCO.

one who talks derisively against them is making a very big mistake.

The most frequent objection to them is that they have come to be regarded in the popular mind as a rival of the regular theatre, by supplying an acceptable substitute for the spoken and acted play at a price so low that the older stage is unable to compete with them.

There has never been a time in the theatre's history when it has not been compelled to meet the rivalry of some newly arisen form of entertainment. Such rivals in the past, however, have been comparatively short-lived, while the motion pictures have undoubtedly come to stay. So the problem they have raised in their relation to the established theatre has caused more speculation and provoked more controversy than any other that the stage has had to deal with before. Of the fear in which they are held by many people of the theatre I find constant evidence, for I am continually being asked whether I see in their enormous popularity either a present menace to the real art of the stage or a future dangerous competitor which may eventually throttle it and take its place

The reason for all this solicitude on the part of the friends of the old dramatic art can be at least partly explained. From their beginning, motion pictures have been attempting not only to compete with the theatre, which came into existence as the home of drama, but even to take actual possession of it. Interest in them, meanwhile, has grown until it seems as if a quarter of the world were now engrossed in the films.

Another quarter, if statistics be reliable, appears to be interested, either directly or indirectly—professionally or financially—in the manufacture of them. If "all the world's a stage" in the classic sense, then all the earth has been turned into a motion-picture studio, according to the prevailing impression.

The question of the relation of the picture shows to the older art of the theatre has never given me much concern. I have watched, though, with friendly and lively interest their onward sweep since the time of the Edison kinetoscope, in 1893, which, I believe, was their first practical demonstration; and by close observation of their development I have sometimes tried to decide in my own mind the artistic ends they may be made to serve. Now, after nearly a quarter of a century, I am still quite as firmly convinced as I ever have been that the fine art of the spoken drama, which has come to us through the centuries, rests upon a much less stable foundation than I would be willing to admit if it is to be dangerously menaced, much less undone, by this additional form of amusement.

Scene from Act II of "The Good Little Devil"

Showing Mary Pickford and Ernest Truex, child actors

David Warfield as Simon Levi in "The Auctioneer"

The first play in which Warfield appeared under Mr. Belasco's management after he left Weber and Fields' Stock Company

THE DRAMA'S FLICKERING BOGY

Motion pictures have not crossed, nor do they threaten to cross, the path of real drama, although as a certain kind of public entertainment they have come into commercial competition with the theatre.

But competition is no new experience for the theatre. The drama of the Greeks and Romans had to compete with the sports and pageantry of the arena for its share of the public's interest. In the seventeenth century the rough pastimes of bear-baiting and cock-fighting claimed to so great an extent the attention of the London populace, which might have witnessed Shakespeare's plays, that laws had to be enacted for the theatre's protection.

Similar conditions have held true right up to the present time. I can easily recall when "The Black Crook" was so hugely popular in New York that there were fears that the regular drama might be superseded. "The Black Crook" was the forerunner of our present elaborately produced musical comedies which now monopolize a large share of every theatrical season; but they have done no harm to the legitimate stage.

All inferior forms of theatrical amusement have been hard hit by the motion pictures, for the very good reason that the pictures often provide more acceptable entertainment at a cheaper price. They have completely swallowed up minstrelsy and practically driven out of existence the cheap stock companies which have been so innocent of all artistic purpose in late years that they have, with few exceptions, not been stock companies at all.

Vaudeville, at the outset, attempted to make use of the screens, but gradually it has become their victim. Managers who try to run their theatres after the manner of co-operative grocery-stores complain that the picture shows have stolen their gallery audiences—which, however, is only one more evidence that the public is not interested in plays written and produced by machine or wholesale methods.

But the legitimately conducted playhouse, in which drama is respected as an art, has not been affected at all, for the reason that motion pictures have drawn a public which was not previously a dependable support of the stage. I am not conscious that my own theatre has in any way been molested by the new conditions, or by the competition which the moving pictures have created, so far as its box-office is concerned. It is, of course, sensitive to dull times, and it is affected during periods of excitement, but I have always found that the public will never ignore a good play.

If any production that I may make contains elements of real interest to theatregoers, I need have no fears of outside influences or competition of any kind. There is no such thing as a menace to the spoken drama when it is actually worthy of attention. It is an imperishable art and it stands alone.

It is unfair to deprecate all motion pictures for the reason that they sometimes pretend to be more than they can ever hope to be. I know of no invention, except printing, which serves a more useful educational purpose. The vivid scenes of the battle-fronts of the European War which they have been supplying to the world of to-day, and will preserve for the world of the future, completely establish their inestimable value. In this field they are outdistancing both the daily press and the magazines. They have robbed the war correspondent of his romantic and adventurous vocation, and literally placed the whole world under fire in the trenches.

Due to motion pictures, also, the study of geography in the school-room is no longer dry nor cold. Every remote wonder of the world has become accessible, through them, to him who travels only in a trolley-car. The Scott and Shackleton Antarctic films planted the South Pole on Broadway. The Rainey pictures of African jungle life narrowed to a few feet the distance which separates us from the equator. It is no longer necessary to accept these far-away regions on faith through the medium of the printed text.

Equally marvelous, and even more valuable-is the camera's aid to science. It records every detail of the most complicated surgical operations. By the simple process of adjusting a microscope to its lens, the infinitesimal bacteria of unseen nature become immediately visible in living, moving forms to the naked eye. Think of an invention by which we may watch a flower unfold from its bulb, or trace the development of a butterfly from its chrysalis!

But wonderful as these feats of the camera are, they deal only with the outward manifestations of things. When motion pictures attempt to go farther and penetrate beneath the surface of life in the effort to analyze and interpret it, they at once establish their limitation. Right here is drawn the line of division which must always separate the screen from the stage and define the difference between the picture show and the acted and spoken play.

This difference between the two mediums is the difference between surface and spirit. Both of them may have an esthetic purpose; but if dramatic art is anything at all, and if it is worthy of being perpetuated, the reason is that it is, above everything else—far above the mere purpose of supplying pleasurable entertainment—an interpretative art which portrays the soul of life. The motion-picture play, on the other hand, has accomplished all of which it is capable when it has reproduced the surface of life; it registers itself in silent images and shadows, while the great vitalizing forces of dramatic art are living personality and the sound of the human voice.

This same living, tangible personality, which gives the spoken and acted drama its subtle power over the human emotions, is no less the secret of the strength of nations. It was the actual, living personality—first that of Kerensky and later that of Lenine — that was the chief driving influence of two successive stages of the Russian Revolution. The real human and personal force of David Lloyd George unified the British Empire in its struggle for the world's democracy. These examples show exactly what I mean and tell the whole story of the difference between motion pictures and the real drama in their effect upon the emotions. Does any one believe that a picture of Lloyd George, silently thrown upon a screen, could inspire great armies to face death?

The relation which the photograph bears to the painted portrait also helps to define the distinction I make between the motion-picture play and the acted drama. A portrait, through the interpretative genius of the painter, reveals the soul of its subject. The photograph can only indicate the subject's physical peculiarities.

No doubt it was thought that a cheap means

had been found to replace the art of the por-
trait-painter when Daguerre, during the first
third of the last century, discovered the process
of photographing a posed image on silver-
plated copper. Since then the science of
photography has made astounding advances.
The picture, which once required several hours
to produce, can now be made in the two-
hundred-and-fiftieth part of a second. Yet
photography has not encroached upon the art
of portrait-painting, and the painter is destined always to remain supreme.

From the time of its invention the hungry
eye of the motion-picture camera has looked
greedily upon the art of the stage. Its very
earliest feat was to reproduce the movements
of a dancing-girl. The theatre, on account of
its architectural arrangement, was instantly
seized as a convenient place for moving-picture
exhibitions.

Also, from their beginning, the effort has
been to exploit motion pictures commercially
as a pendant of the drama. Acted plays were
appropriated because they furnished ready-
made material for screen shows. Trained performers of the theatre became valuable to the
operators of the films because it was profitable
to trade upon their well-advertised reputations
before a new public. Without the exertion of
creative effort, plots of popular novels could
be worked over into scenarios.

Thus, from their very outset, except when they have been devoted to reproducing scenes from nature, motion pictures have been a parasite feeding upon the arts of the theatre. Far from attempting to invent their own medium of expression, they have been content either to imitate or to borrow. These and many other circumstances have tended to establish in the public mind a false relationship between the stage and the screen.

If the motion pictures ever hope to challenge the regular drama seriously, they must evolve some form of art distinctly their own, and educate their performers in an entirely new technique. They cannot always be satisfied with the cast-offs of the older theatre.

Up to the present time no writer has been found who can apply life to a scenario in such a way that it can be silently interpreted by actors who have been trained to the methods of the spoken drama. I have often been told that performing before the camera is a good experience for our actors; but that is a mistaken notion, for the reason that the spoken dialogue of a regular play sets in motion the mental processes in the imagined characters which are translated to an audience in the players' actions.

For instance, the motion-picture performer is told by his director to assume the appearance and pose of thinking. But just what shall he be thinking about? In a spoken drama that mental action would be the spontaneous result of the situation in which the character is placed, plus the equally spontaneous effect of what the other characters on the stage are saying and doing. Before the camera, on the other hand, the player has nothing to think about except the director's instructions. The result of such a process can be only to make the poser artificial, unnatural, and mechanical, and this is precisely the fault I detect in the acting of even the best directed motion-picture plays.

I do not mean that there is nothing in motion-picture plays to stir the imagination or appeal to the emotions of spectators, but when I have examined them closely to discover the source of such effect I have invariably found that it was in the story rather than in the acting.

The inspiration which always manifests itself in good interpretations of characters in the regular theatre is necessarily absent from the plays of the screens, because the acting must be done in a studio without the presence of an audience. Applause is tonic and elixir to the actor. It is one of the psychological phenomena of the theatre, as every one who has seen a rehearsal of a play before empty seats must be aware.

The actor lives on approbation. That is why

the people of the theatre, throughout its whole history, have been willing to make such great sacrifices for their art. There is something in the magnetic influence of an audience's presence which thrills the actor and puts the spark of life into his work. Without it, no matter how great may be his zeal, his performance takes on that flat and inspirationless aspect which I invariably notice in the motion-picture plays.

To help counteract these disadvantages of what I may call studio acting, motion-picture plays must be limited to expressing only the obvious and elementary things in life. Whatever appeal the performers make to their spectators must depend upon physical attractiveness. The heroine must invariably be beautiful. The hero must be cast in the mold of an Apollo. So long as the main figures of any scenario have to rely upon physical attributes to render them impressive, neglecting the soul for the sake of the shell, motion-picture plays cannot by any pretext enter the field of an art which has for its fundamental purpose the interpretation of life.

Many of our best actors who have attempted the pictures have proved to be failures. The complaint of the directors against them is that they "fail to register." But that is not what the directors really mean. The secret of their failure is that they have actually succeeded in registering some of the passions of human nature, which is exactly what the directors and movie-lovers, either consciously or unconsciously, do not want them to do.

Deep emotions, when they are faithfully expressed, tend to distort the features and intensify the facial lines. Therefore, a correct portrayal of passion does not conform to the standard of sightliness which has been set for the screens. On the other hand, some little nonentity, who may not have the remotest appreciation of the emotion that is involved, might in the same character prove entirely satisfactory.

When all this artificiality ceases and scenes and characters are played for what they are worth, the motion-picture dramas will improve accordingly. As they are now, they suggest to me only a beautiful corpse—a thing without life.

It must be a comparatively easy matter to accomplish motion pictures as they are now done. The best proof of it is the great number of corporations engaged in their production, the hundreds of quickly arisen directors employed in staging them, and the thousands —perhaps tens of thousands—of men and women who have suddenly blossomed into performers. As the profession develops it will become smaller, because it will impose requirements upon its people which cannot be so easily met.

A convincing proof that something is now lacking in the pictures from the viewpoint of drama is the fact that when they set out to make their strongest impression upon their spectators they must mass great crowds. The maneuvering of large bodies of rushing figures against picturesque natural landscapes is their top notch. Thus, their best work falls under the classification of spectacle, which is a primitive and inferior form of drama. To advance artistically they must follow a new path toward simpler things.

I feel positive that this advance will never come until motion-picture plays find a way to interpret themselves without relying on outside aids. There can be no art in them so long as their scenes must be interrupted every minute or two in order to let an audience know what the story is all about. Scenario-writers will have to devise a means to develop their plots without mottoes, "cut-backs," and similar devices which they now use to serve as reminders of past episodes or to give emphasis to the scene in hand. The scheme of flashing back momentarily on the screen an earlier episode to warn an audience "lest we forget" had, at first, certain advantages, but the present excessive use of the device has made it monotonous. Its effect is always to destroy the artistic symmetry of both story and acting.

When motion pictures free themselves of

such clumsy, haphazard methods as these, directors will engage and rehearse their companies as carefully as producers in the regular theatre now do. It would be a good thing for them to begin at once to work on this idea, for it might lead to screen dramas which really mean something.

II

One comment I have made regarding motion pictures, so far as they have affected the established form of drama, is open to dispute and, therefore, calls for qualification. I have said I am not conscious that the additional amusement they have brought into the world has menaced, so far as its material prosperity is concerned, my theatre or any other theatre in which drama is produced as an art rather than as a commodity for commercial speculation. In other words, the public comes in as great numbers as ever before to see a genuinely good play. But I admit—and this is the qualification to my former observation—that the pictures are interfering vexatiously with the work that goes on behind theatre curtains.

The problem they have raised is not commercial. It touches only the artistic aims of the regular dramatic director; and it grows, I find, every time I set out to produce a new play.

The new field which motion-picture shows

have opened has attracted great numbers of our actors, who find that by capitalizing the prestige they have won on the dramatic stage they can earn in the studios, in a few weeks, more money than they could command in the theatre in an entire season. As a rule, they profess to regard the screens contemptuously, especially if they are sure of their standing in the older art, and they place their demands for salary high accordingly.

They know that the motion-picture directors can afford to pay, because it needs only a few weeks at the most to make a picture. There the expense ends and the money begins to flow in. In my theatre, on the other hand, the $30,000 I may invest in a production is only a bare beginning. So long as the play remains before the public I am put to an average additional expense of $8,000 a week to maintain it.

This kind of competition—competition for actors, not for audiences—has placed a severe handicap upon producers who are careful how they organize their companies and cast their plays. There was a time when hordes of applicants for jobs were lined up at my stage entrance or in the waiting-room outside my office door. I find fewer of them there now, and they are not so eager for the positions they once so greatly coveted.

Sometimes I have engaged a young woman

to impersonate a maid, or a young man for the rôle of a butler. Such inconspicuous parts do not demand much ability, yet the salary I am willing to pay would, in any other profession, be preposterously large. Yet the next day these actors have asked to be released from their contracts, claiming that they have been offered $200 a week to pose in a picture show. I may resent this sort of inconstancy, but usually I am forced to let them go, because a dissatisfied actor is almost fatal to a well-produced play.

The regular theatre's new vexations do not end with the trained actors who secede temporarily to perform for the screen. The motion-picture shows are also diverting every year from the stage profession hundreds of young people who, if they entered it and began at the foot of the ladder, might develop positive genius. They are attracted into the other field because it looks easier, and is much easier, than the profession of the legitimate actor.

They know that vocal training is not needed by the picture player. They are aware that youth and beauty are more valuable than experience for the purposes of the screens. They like the idea of doing their acting in the open air, for a great many of the scenes in motion-picture plays are shown in natural surroundings. The jobs they get may be of short duration, but there are many to be had, and the pay is generally high. So they cannot be blamed for choosing the path of least resistance.

Nevertheless, it is regretable that so many young men and women, perhaps with potential ability, should select a career that ignores all need of the preliminary study essential to the development of an artist. They are lost to the regular dramatic profession, for, once a moving-picture actor, always a moving-picture actor.

I have been asked time and again if I believe an occasional "flier in the movies" to be harmful to the people of the regular dramatic profession. If they be actors of just ordinary—that is to say, undistinguished—talent, I do not think it injures their work, provided such excursions are not undertaken too often.

At the same time, I can invariably detect a player who has been performing for the screens. He betrays himself in his constant tendency to strike rigid poses, in his care to emphasize—or "register"—each changing expression, and in his effort to present either a full face or a profile to the audience. He is likely, also, in various unconscious ways, to be artificial and mechanical in his gestures.

If an actor of such ordinary ability, however, should ask my advice about accepting an engagement in the pictures, I would say to him:

"Do not attempt to ride two horses. Be either a legitimate actor or a motion-picture actor. If you think you have talent for the regular theatre, cling to it. Do not dilute your experience in the one with experiments in the other. The person who tries to ride two horses falls between them in the end. Motion pictures are a world distinct from the regular drama. No one who aspires to be an artist can hope to inhabit both."

I would try to impress upon my questioner that the established drama will not change. We of the regular theatre are always on the lookout for the kind of genius that gives life to the characters conceived in the playwright's imagination. The really able actor will always be lauded and demanded by the public. It lies within the power of his genius to revitalize the comedies and tragedies of all ages. We are now in a period of light plays in the theatre, but a Booth, if he were newly arisen and in sympathy with the present methods of the stage, could make "Hamlet" live a year on Broadway. This being true, why should any one fear for the future of the theatre's art or try to discourage the popularity of the motion pictures?

Every now and then, though, comes along some person of a peculiar type who seems to me to be gifted by nature to act for the motion pictures. Such men or women, even under the most favorable conditions, would be likely to find only limited success in the regular theatre. Douglas Fairbanks, with his breezy, healthy, out-of-door personality, athletic prowess, and daredevil proclivities, is the best example of this peculiar type. Something in the gentle, sweetly sentimental personality of Mary Pickford exactly qualifies her to act for the screens. Her direct antithesis, but suited not less well for the shadow vampires who nowadays are dear to every movie fan's heart, is that sinuous priestess of the obvious, Theda Bara. To such as these I would say:

"Go into the movies and remain in them. There you will find the field of greatest success and profit for yourselves and of your largest usefulness to the amusement world. In you there has been born the instinct for the screens."

A very different situation arises when an established star of the regular theatre is tempted by the inducements which the motion-picture managers are perpetually dangling before him. His step from the studio to the stage may be of grave consequence, not only for him, but for the theatre. To have become a star in the real sense means that the actor has reached the first rank in his profession, and something more. It implies not only the superlative ability which distinguishes his work from that of other players, but also an exceptional personal appeal to a wide public, which

is the result of God-given qualities that few
other actors possess.

When a star with these unusual endowments
is asked to cast his radiance upon the screen,
he should reflect that to become an idol of
the movie crowd will inevitably destroy the
finer personal appeal which he can count as
one of his most reliable and permanent assets
in the legitimate theatre. An audience which
can see for five cents a great celebrity soon
does not care to see him at all.

The number of the theatre's real stars is
small. They are in such great demand and
so well paid for their work that they are the
most independent of all artists. They enjoy a
prestige with the legitimate theatre's public
which they cannot afford to endanger, even
for the extravagant salaries which motion
pictures offer. I would counsel them to be
wary and keep out, for the compensation of the
screens is not a sufficient return, however
large, for what they will be asked to give.

The great star who goes into the pictures
also risks his professional reputation, for the
reason that the camera affords him only a
limited medium in which to employ his abilities. He may discover, after it is too late,
that the equipment which served him best on
the regular stage is useless for the restricted
purposes of the screens. I could name a score
of such stars who have failed outright when

Probably the Best Picture of David Warfield as Anton von
Barwig in "The Music Master"

they have attempted to perform before the camera, and whose only value to the picture-producer was their well-advertised fame. To offset this story of unwisely directed effort I could also name half a hundred pretty nonentities who have literally triumphed in motion pictures without knowledge of more than the bare elementary principles of the acting art.

My stars have not yet been ambitious to make the adventure in the motion-picture world. I might not oppose them if they should become seized with the desire. But I count it fortunate for me, as well as for them, that they value the stage's art sufficiently to remain loyal to it, despite the huge salaries which I, as well as they, know they might earn.

The great number of enterprises which the popularity of motion pictures has encouraged is also levying a heavy toll upon the regular theatre's always limited number of competent stage directors. This phase of the problem which the picture shows have raised cannot hamper seriously the theatre manager who is capable of directing the staging of his own productions, though it must be annoying to the new generation of managers whose qualifications are restricted to the supervision of the theatre's business affairs.

Like the actors, the stage directors have been led to the pictures by the better financial inducements they can offer, and some of them, who might never have risen high in the regular theatre, have shown surprising aptitude in the newer field. I think that this is the most attractive work that motion pictures can offer. Since they have not progressed beyond the experimental stage, their possibilities are many for the director who has inventive ability and original ideas.

The director in this country who has accomplished most for the motion pictures is David W. Griffith. His ability to handle massed crowds amounts to positive genius, and he has raised the picture spectacle to what I believe to be its highest point of interest. His stage knows no linear limitations. The field of his operations extends as far as the eye can see.

Mr. Griffith's entrance into the pictures was the result of a lucky accident. I had known him as a young actor out West when the invention of the camera was practically new, and he had applied to me for a position in one of my dramatic companies. I had none to offer him at that time, so he joined the Vitagraph Company, first as a screen actor. Almost immediately he showed special gifts in the directing branch of the business, and from that time his rise continued steadily until finally he has reached the top.

I have always been interested in his progress and have watched each new step in his accomplishments with increasing admiration. He

is destined to go much farther in his field,
but his future advancement will come only
when he gives up complicated pictures and
adopts a simpler form for the screen show.
All motion pictures, in fact, will come into a
closer relation with art when they choose more
intimate themes, devote more attention to the
detailed development of their stories, and
place less reliance upon stars.

I have never felt an ambition to direct a
motion-picture play, but I have often thought
of the process I would adopt if I were to undertake such a task. It would be greatly at
variance with the methods now followed in the
studios, but I wager I would obtain good
results.

I would select a very human story adjusted
to the simplest backgrounds, with very few
characters and no ensemble whatever. In
inventing the "business" of the scenes I would
contrive to have the hero or heroine hold the
stage alone whenever possible; for I would
aim to tell the story, not by a correlation of
incidents, but by the facial expressions of the
actors. Experience in my own theatre has
convinced me that nothing is so calculated to
command the interest of an audience as the
concentration of a scene upon the work of one
performer.

I would avoid the use of "cut-backs,"
"close-ups," and the other cumbersome and

disconcerting devices now in vogue on the screens. And I would never consider my picture fit for public exhibition so long as it had to be interrupted by captions of explanation. A motion-picture play which must depend on mottoes to communicate its meaning to the spectator is suitable only to be thrown away. As on my regular stage, I would scrutinize every scene closely to discover distracting, confusing, or reiterated points, and these I would contrive to remove.

Rehearsals would be continued until the actors were able to go through their rôles without prompting or directing of any kind, and when it came to the filming process I would insist that the scenes should be photographed consecutively and in the order of their development. This last detail I would consider the most important feature of my method, since by following it out I am sure I could show the mental processes of the characters which so seldom now are even suggested in motion-picture plays.

It is a fatal error of the motion-picture director to photograph the opening scene of a screen drama a week, perhaps, after the final scene has been made. In the regular theatre a play works up to its biggest scene by degrees. The actor, also, rises gradually to his great dramatic moment. This is the natural process by which the mind and the emotions work, and there is no reason why it should not be followed in acting before the camera. I am positive that the absence of inspiration and imagination from even the best of the motion-picture plays up to the present time is because directors have fallen into the habit, for reasons of economy or convenience, of doing their work in patches.

My picture being now complete and ready for the public, I would require that the speed of its exhibition be regulated to fit the natural gestures and movements of human beings. In all the picture plays I have ever seen the figures dash through the scenes with such lightning rapidity that every facial expression becomes a grimace, and the effect of the whole is turned into travesty. Nothing in the motion-picture profession is quite so appalling to me as this malicious energy of the camera man.

If, in these observations concerning a comparatively new medium of entertainment and its relation to the spoken and acted drama, to which my life has been devoted, I have combined criticism with suggestion, it is not because I underrate the pleasure it now affords for a vast public or the possibilities its development promises for the future. The motion picture better deserves commendation for what it has already accomplished than blame because its necessary limitations deny it a place among the theatre's allied arts. Those who regard the picture play lightly because they cannot derive from it the artistic satisfaction which they find in real drama, make the mistake of demanding too much of it. They should remember that one cannot be confused with the other, for the reason that drama is life and the screen is destined always to remain a cold picture of life.

But there is no reason, in view of the mechanical perfection of the camera, why it should not develop an art of its own, or, at least, something which is akin to art. That art will not appear until the motion picture has developed a separate medium which does not borrow from the acted and spoken drama, has found its own school of writers, and trained its own kind of actors.

I would not be surprised if the time were to come when motion-picture directors, profiting by the experience of the regular stage, will organize permanent companies of their own and train their actors according to entirely new methods. Then they will shun the people of the regular stage, for the reason that they will require an entirely different theory of acting.

When such a readjustment of the picture plays is made, it will be time enough for producers in the regular theatre to fear the competition of the screens. Until then pictures will remain only the theatre's bogyman—things without substance and made of shadows. Even afterward they can never actually menace the older art, for they will still be denied the vital element of all drama—the human voice.

I have never heard the claim made in Latin countries that pantomime is a menace to the real theatre, though it has existed there for centuries as a separate art. I have never known the marionette theatres to be regarded as dangerous competitors of the real theatre, though they are, or were, more numerous in southern Europe than the movie shows are in America. Like the pictures, they are an additional amusement in a world which will forever crave and demand amusement.

The theatre in which I live and work can never be endangered from the outside. There is nothing which can actually menace it or divert from it the public's sustaining interest, except bad plays and bad actors. For these, fortunately, the remedy lies in its own hands.

Chapter VII

HOLDING THE MIRROR UP TO NATURE

I

THROUGHOUT the history of the theatre there has never been a period of considerable duration when it has not seemed as if destructive agencies were subtly at work to swerve the art which it shelters, and of which it is the symbol, away from the clearly defined pathway of normal, healthy development.

These iconoclastic movements or tendencies have not been confined to the Anglo-Saxon theatre or to any one era. Their disrupting influence has been exerted alike against the theatre of France, of Germany, of Italy, and of Spain, and, at a later time, when art in Scandinavia and Russia began to find its expression in drama, against the theatre of these peoples as well. Nowhere in the world has the theatre remained immune from the experimenter with fantastic notions and limited experience who has sought to deflect its progress from its normal course. The ancient

avid Belasco and His Mother,
Reina Martin Belasco

David Belasco at Twenty
Taken in 1873. Photo by White
Studio

avid Belasco at Thirty-two
Taken in 1885. Photo by Falk

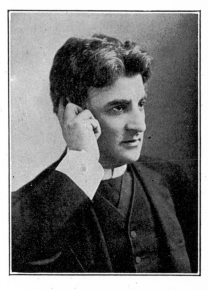

David Belasco at Forty
Taken about 1893. Photo by Sarony

Robert T. Haines as Kara, Blanche Bates as Yo-San, in
"The Darling of the Gods"

theatre of Athens and Rome was similarly afflicted; I have no doubt that the still more ancient theatre of China and Japan bore its share also of the burden laid upon it by the revolutionist, the charlatan, and, by what is still worse, the misguided enthusiast who has not been able to interpret clearly the records of the past or to profit by the truths of his own time.

This very human impulse to meddle with the drama, and to substitute for the accepted standards of the theatre fantastic practices which are only fads and whims of the passing hour, has not been restricted to any one of the allied departments of its art. Such standards have not been hastily formed. They are created out of the brilliant and sound traditions which have been bequeathed to the stage by its greatest geniuses who have gone before and whose accomplishments have formed the successive steps in its progress.

Every department of the art has been affected temporarily by such pernicious and destructive interference. The golden age of dramatic poetry in the Anglo-Saxon theatre of the seventeenth century—the age of Shakespeare—was followed by an interval when it seemed that the English stage was doomed to destruction by a wave of licentiousness. Yet it survived the playwrights of that time, and retrieved itself with the sparkling, brilliant comedies of manners of the eighteenth century. The wave of fustian, spread by the flamboyant dramatists of the early nineteenth century, was swept away by a school of playwrights within the memory of a still living generation, which sought again to hold a truer mirror up to nature and to reflect life faithfully on the stage. Is there not even to-day a certain temptation to readjust the technique of dramatic construction to the newly evolved principles of the motion-picture plays? Will it last? Must the standards established by our permanent dramatic literature go for nothing? I think not.

So, too, in the art of acting. Periods of upheaval have come when acting has degenerated to strutting, posturing, and oratory. But the human spark in the histrionic art has remained alive in defiance of the innovators.

The arts of costuming and stage decoration, too, have passed through their times of revolution, but always the best that tradition affords has survived. The pictorial side of the theatre has kept pace with the drama's normal development, appropriating and adjusting to its needs the inventions and discoveries of the scientific world, and always bringing the stage a little closer to its goal—the faithful reflection of nature.

Consider this development in the art of lighting alone, which I believe to be of greater importance in enforcing the meaning and the appeal of a work of dramatic art than either scenery or costumes. The crude rushlights of Shakespeare's time were followed successively by the tallow and sperm candles, the oil-lamp, gas, the calcium, and finally by electricity in all its various and intricate uses. Each method improved upon the one which had preceded it; each brought the stage a little nearer to a more faithful suggestion of the effects of nature.

But with such improvements, have we been expected to cast aside the established truths of the influence of light upon the human emotions? Nature told the dramatist and the stage director of centuries ago, as it tells him to-day, that romantic love suggests twilight or moonlight scenes, that joyousness and gaiety are best expressed in sunlight, that sorrow makes its most poignant appeal when shown in subdued lights, and that the sinister and the ugly are intensified when revealed in uncertain shadows.

The circumstance that the theatre and its art in all times and in all countries have been made a target for extravagant innovations by theorists and irresponsible experimenters is not, to my mind, very remarkable. In the very nature of the theatre lie reasons why it should be an inviting field for the faddist and for those others even of sincere purpose who are possessed of the mistaken idea that their newly conceived notions of its art are superior to the accumulated traditions of the centuries. These reasons, though, do not deny the theatre the right to progress along the line of its normal development.

Of all the fine arts, the dramatic art responds most generally and directly to the desires and tastes of the people. Of all the fine arts, it stands in most intimate relation to their daily lives. The theatre, whatever be the present system of its management, is a public institution, and it and its affairs are continually in the public eye. The worker within its walls is certain of an audience such as the worker in no other art commands. And actual accomplishment in the dramatic art receives its reward more quickly and more generously than similar accomplishment in any of its sister arts.

It is inevitable, therefore, that an institution which has such a firm grip upon public interest should entice both the well-meaning innovator, with false theories of art to exploit, and the faddist and crank who is chiefly intent upon seeking notoriety for himself. There are also freaks and revolutionaries in the other arts, but the incentive to them is not so great, since their work is not performed in the limelight of public attention. And those who make the theatre the scene of fantastic experiments may always rely to a certain extent upon the curiosity which is inherent in the public.

So the irresponsible experimenter in the theatre rarely fails to command an audience, temporarily, and the more energetically he proclaims his freak innovations the larger, for a limited time, his audience becomes. A crowd can always be summoned to inspect an exhibit of freakish art, just as it will gather to gaze with wonder upon a five-legged calf, although none in the crowd may be willing to concede that the one is good art or that the other is a good kind of calf. In the mean time, however, the exhibitor is accomplishing his purpose, for at least he is attracting the crowd.

It is inevitable, also, that the theatre be sensitive to the thought, movements, and proclivities of its own time. The stage is a mirror in which are reflected the manners and peculiarities of life of its contemporaneous day. So the drama is always affected to a large degree by the thought and by the social, political, and economic customs of the generation from which it springs. Much of such drama is ephemeral and transitory, and soon disappears; but that part of it which is permanent and survives becomes the epitome of its own era. So it is understandable that it should reflect, fitfully, at least, all the freakish extremes of its time, as well as all normal lines of artistic endeavor.

It is one of the fortunate peculiarities of the theatre, nevertheless, that, to whatever lengths its extremes and extravagances may go, they never fail to provide in good time their own antidote. The pendulum of its activities swings first this way and then that, but invariably it returns to its normal position, and this position marks the path of its healthy progress.

For this steadying influence which seems to lie within the theatre there is an easy explanation. Of all the arts the dramatic art is the most democratic in its appeal. Its craftsmen who contribute to its real dignity and permanency must be guided, not by the eccentricities of the self-appointed intellectual few, but by the normal (which, in the long run, are the best balanced) tastes and desires of the great general public.

To this vast community of the theatre's supporters the book of nature is never closed. They need no extraordinary faculty of perception to detect to what extent the great truths of life and nature are faithfully reproduced in their dramas. Their knowledge of life has been gained from their experience with life, their appreciation of the beauty of nature from nature itself as it unfolds around them. The emerald green of the fields, the cerulean blue of the sky, the changing hues of a summer sunset, the harmonious mingling of colors in a distant landscape—these manifestations of nature are familiar to all people through actual experience. They refuse to be deluded by the distorted forms and colors contrived by those who look out upon the world through abnormal eyes. The mirror which reflects nature to them in the theatre must be neither concave nor convex. Its illusion must be true, and only to the extent that it is true will it successfully stir their imaginations. So, again, the freak movements in scenic art which spring up from time to time do not divert the stage from its normal course, even though temporarily they may tend to retard its progress.

As I have full confidence in the steadying influence of the healthy taste of the great public which supports the theatre, I have never been much disturbed by the sporadic eccentricities of which the stage has been made the victim. Through thirty-seven, or more, years of constant and intimate association with the theatre, and as a producer of plays, I have witnessed these vagaries within the theatre, and the waves of temporary encouragement they have received from the public, come and go. I have seen the pendulum swing wide, but always it has returned to the center. There have been times when it has seemed as if the stage had surrendered itself to the study of problems of sex abnormality, but always it has reverted to the normal truths of nature. Again, it has seemed as if false and exaggerated romance had stifled the expression of real life in the drama, but presently the common sense of the public has returned and truth has reasserted itself. Life is various, and human nature, to be faithfully depicted, must be shown in all its aspects. I have never doubted the power of the theatre to maintain its even balance, to be true to life from which it derives its inspiration, and it has been the single aim of all my work and thought to bring the theatre and the dramatic art into closer and truer harmony with life and nature. Through such effort, and only through such effort, on the part of those who are in control of the stage will the theatre continue to maintain its place of interest and influence among the people, and the drama preserve its integrity among the arts—the greatest of the arts because it combines them all.

I must admit, however, that sometimes I have had not a few misgivings because of a comparatively recent form of theatrical eccentricity which masquerades as extreme impressionism and which, after spasmodic outbreaks, principally in the theatres of Germany, has found champions among a few writers—seldom practical men of the theatre—in England and also in this country. I have little doubt that, like all other faddish movements in the theatre, this vagary, too, will have its little day and then disappear. I do not fear its ultimate ill effect upon our dramatic art, but I do deplore its possible influence for a time upon the viewpoint and taste of a considerable part of the theatregoing public who should be the most ardent champions of legitimate endeavor in the dramatic profession.

This school of impressionism is avowedly hostile to naturalism—the art of reflecting life and nature in their true and normal aspects, either through the proscenium opening of the theatre or upon the canvas of the painter— and as a lover of nature who sees beauty through normal eyes, and draws all his inspirations from it, I would be unfaithful to my ideals if I did not raise my voice in protest. Its champions argue that impressionism is revolutionizing all existing forms of dramatic production. Let us see. In Germany, where before the war it claimed its greatest number of adherents, where Max Reinhardt, the Berlin producer, is its oracle, it is only casual. Mr. Reinhardt has earned the compliment of inspiring many imitators, but, of the two theatres he directs, one is restricted entirely to dramas produced by established methods, while he devotes the other to his fantastic experiments with impressionistic draperies. Warsaw, Moscow, and St. Petersburg each has had a small "art" theatre given over to these stage experiments. The movement has also claimed a few adherents in Paris, but there it has been a pronounced failure; it has hardly so much as tinged the art of the French stage. London has had its voluble mouthpiece in Gordon Craig, who has accomplished little more than to ventilate his fantastic theories in an inexplicable book, entitled *On the Art of the Theatre.* He certainly has not succeeded in dimming the luster of Sir Henry Irving as a commanding genius among British actors and producers, or Alma-Tadema as a genius of the scene designer's brush.

The gospel preached and tiresomely reiterated by experimenters in this method of production would lead us to believe that the theatre and the acting art, as they have developed from the Elizabethan age, are all wrong. They would have us think that the naturalistic methods of decorating the stage have the effect of stifling instead of stirring imagination. They would urge that the faithful imitation of the effects of nature, as an environment for characters in the living images of men and women, is destructive to real beauty and truth.

But are they? Must the thought and labor of the geniuses of the theatre through the centuries go for nothing? Have we, in the present day, learned nothing from the past? Have the great personages of the English and American theatre—Garrick, Kean, Macready, Forrest, Charlotte Cushman, Wallack, Benson, Irving, Daly—to mention only a scattered few in a formidable list, lived in vain? Are the works of our dramatists in the last generation, who have brought the stage elbow to elbow with life, to be discarded and left to molder on the shelves because the characters of men and women which they have portrayed cannot be represented in the theatre according to the eccentricities of impressionistic art? Is Sir Arthur Wing Pinero's "The Second Mrs. Tanqueray," the most vital and truest picture of human experience, and the most perfect model of social drama in its decade, to be no longer available for the uses of the actor and stage-manager? If it is, how can its realism be represented before fantastic curtains and upon a stage so constructed that the actors are practically in the audience? How would the impressionistic stage director, for instance, produce Henry Arthur Jones's "The Silver King" or the virile, naturalistic drama of Augustus Thomas?

It is the claim of the radical impressionists that to reproduce the effects of nature faithfully in the theatre is to stifle imagination and to distract attention from the beauty of the spoken word of the play. It is argued that a few violent splotches of green upon a drapery can better express to an audience the idea of a forest than the actual reproduction in painting, and in light effects, of that forest. Or that a few vivid, solid colors spread over an unstable back-cloth can suggest to the mind the brilliant glories of a summer sunset. I confess that I cannot follow the theories of theatrical impressionism to such lengths.

By those who admire naturalism in the theatre I have been called a magician and a hypnotist. By those who subscribe to fantastical stage decoration I am charged, on the other hand, with being an unimaginative and unsympathetic realist. Both charges are the sheerest nonsense! I gained my first ideas of lighting from the wonderful skies of southern California. I went direct to nature for my inspiration. There, on the brightest days, I would sit among the hills and watch the lights and shadows as they came and went. After a time I began trying to reproduce those lights and shadows. I loved it all, and I knew I could not go wrong, for my lessons were learned from the book of nature. How, may I ask, can one be false to art when he is true to nature, which is God's work?

Mere conventional effects in the theatre are not true to nature or authentic in the impression they make upon the imagination of an audience. For instance, effects of sunlight vary in different localities on the earth. The color qualities of a California sunset are not the same as of a sunset in Japan. Or of a sunset in Mexico. Or among the hills of Alsace-Lorraine. So the processes by which I created the light effects in "The Girl of the Golden West" had to be different from the processes which I used in securing corresponding effects in "The Darling of the Gods." And the soft light with which I flooded the scene through the convent's open door in the production of "Marie-Odile" differed from either of the other two.

I have been applauded for what I have accomplished in these plays. I fear I have been applauded more than I have deserved, for it is not I who dictated their light effects, but nature. All I had to do was to go to nature for my inspiration and ideas, and then find a way to reproduce accurately nature's phenomena on my stage. And yet I am told that all this is not art, that art consists of pink and yellow and blue splotches upon a curtain, or draperies illuminated from above by shafts of white electric light. I reply that when you use false lights and colors you do not stimulate imagination, you only distort reality. And when you distort reality you have destroyed truth.

II

I have been asked many times what I consider my most successful achievement in stir-

ring imagination through the agencies of
scenery. I invariably reply that the scene
of the passing of an entire night in "Madame
Butterfly" has been my most successful effort
in appealing to the imaginations of those who
have sat before my stage. In that scene the
little Japanese heroine is waiting with her
child for its father, Lieutenant Pinkerton, to
come from the American ship. Her vigil
represented an entire night. To portray this
episode, Blanche Bates was compelled to hold
the stage for fourteen minutes without uttering
a word. So, to keep an audience's imagination
stirred—to persuade it that what it was wit-
nessing was real—it was necessary to have a
scene of changing beauty. There was not a
dissenting voice in the criticism of that scene.
My experiment was hazardous, but it succeeded, and its success was due entirely to its
imaginative appeal. The secret of its fascination lay in my use of lights.

Let me also cite the scene of the bamboo
forest in "The Darling of the Gods," in which
Kara and his band of Samurai, driven to their
last stand, fulfil the highest ideal of ancient
Japanese chivalry and end their lives by hara-
kiri. My problem was to impress the awful-
ness of this situation upon my audiences and
yet eliminate from it every repellent or grue-
some detail. So, behind the gaunt bamboo-
trees I conceived a great, crimson moon,

indicative of blood and death. The Samurai were lost to view back among the bamboo-trees. Then, as Yo-San and Kara waited in their last love embrace, one heard the clatter of falling armor as each of the band went to his self-chosen sacrifice.

The effect of this scene, and I base my opinion upon the demeanor of hundreds of audiences that I have watched, was electrical. And yet, sixteen years after "The Darling of the Gods" was produced, I am informed by a new school of perhaps two dozen enthusiasts that naturalism has become an outlaw among the arts.

I may offer one more instance in the production of Edward Knoblock's drama, "Marie-Odile." It supplies a good contrast between the new stagecraft and the methods of realism to which I shall adhere as long as I remain in the service of dramatic art.

When the Prussian Uhlans have invaded the convent, from which all the nuns have fled, except the little novice who is the heroine of the play, and are seated at the table where the audience had seen the nuns sitting at breakfast before, their singing of "The Watch on the Rhine" is interrupted by the command of the sergeant, who calls out:

"Silence! Silence! Didn't you hear something? Listen! I—thought—I—heard—guns. 'Sh! Don't you?"

They all listened intently, and the corporal, who had gone over to the doorway leading to the courtyard, says:

"Yes—'way off.   I thought just now—"

This little scene was so impressively performed and it stirred to such a degree the imagination of the audience that a vivid impression was conveyed of actually hearing the distant booming of cannon.   Yet not a single gun had been heard.   All was silence on the stage.

Now it would have been very easy for me to fire a gun, or guns, muffled to suggest distance.   But I did not want actual noise to mar the sustained quiet and serenity of the play. So I was obliged to make the audience believe that they had heard the guns, even though they actually had not.

To accomplish this purpose required extraordinarily careful drilling of the actors.   Over and over again during the rehearsals of the play, when the lines, such as "Silence! Silence! Didn't you hear something?   Listen!   I— thought—I—heard—guns!" were spoken, a muffled drum in the distance, off-stage, was beaten in imitation of the far-off discharge of cannon.   I kept this up day after day until the soldiers became so accustomed to actually hearing the sounds that, when the drum was taken away, its sound was thoroughly transplanted into their imaginations.   Such became the imagination of the scene itself that it stirred equally the imaginations of the people in the audience. Can it, therefore, be contended with truth that the quality of imagination, for which the real artist must forever strive in the theatre, does not enter the method by which the realist in dramatic art goes about his task?

The new method of stagecraft places altogether too much importance upon the producer. I hear a good deal about "the Belasco method," and I suppose it originates from the importance and emphasis I place upon every minute detail which makes for truth in my theatre. And as a producer I have always attained my best results when I have succeeded in keeping all eccentricity out of my productions. On the other hand, stage impressionism is most striking and effective when the producer dominates the scene at the expense of the play.

The producer, after all, is only the third party in the presentation of a drama. Before him come both the author and the actors. The producer must be content to be only the unseen interpreter who directs the actors and, by the environment which he provides, creates the atmosphere which is in complete harmony with the essence and feeling of the play. On the other hand, in the fantastic productions of the impressionistic school of dramatic art, the producer is invariably an intruder in the play.

When I read of the accomplishments of the innovators who are striving to upset the established standards of dramatic art, I sometimes wonder if the entire architecture and arrangement of our theatres must be changed. Is there to be no place left for a new Pinero? Must every play of the future be a burlesque or a fable? Or is life to continue to be reflected as it is and as normal observers of its manifold complexities know it?

I confess I am just a little astounded at some of the "discoveries" which these innovators claim to have made. One of these is that, in the instances of certain plays, footlights are destructive to illusion and that, therefore, they should not be used. These revolutionary improvements, and they include the double stage, are said to have originated in Europe. I would suggest that there should be a little praise for what we have done in this country.

It has been, for a quarter of a century, my practice to do away with footlights whenever the artistic needs of my productions have demanded it. More than twenty-five years ago, when I produced "The Rajah" at the old Madison Square Theatre, I presented entire scenes without the use of footlights. It happens also that the old Madison Square Theatre, since torn down, was equipped with the first

double stage in the world—the invention of
Steele Mackaye, who was an American genius
in the theatre.

Before I owned my own theatre, when I
was still occupying playhouses under lease, I
was compelled to improvise a means of covering
the footlight space along the edge of the stage
when I made productions the artistic needs
of which demanded other methods of illumination than footlights. So usual had become my
practice of doing away with these lights that,
when I built the present Belasco Theatre, I
had a device invented under my supervision
by which the footlights would automatically
sink below the level of the flooring. This
arrangement gave me an opportunity to make
another innovation in stage construction, the
need of which I had long appreciated. Simul-
taneously with the sinking of the footlights,
an "apron" would project, widening the
stage over the orchestra pit. This projection
brought my stage in close conformity with
the "platform" stage of which, latterly, I
have been hearing so much. It not only afforded more room for my actors, but also
secured greater intimacy of relationship between them and my audiences.

These innovations demanded improved
means of lighting in other parts of the stage,
so I installed a newly invented apparatus for
overhead and side lighting. I had come to

realize long before this time that rays of light, shot upward from footlights, cast false shadows, under certain conditions, upon the faces of the actors. Such unillusory effects I sought to neutralize by my overhead lights, and I am sure that I succeeded. But since then I have superseded the overhead and side-lighting apparatus with a new system of refracting lights which has brought me nearer to the effects for which I have been striving.

I did not extinguish my footlights in the first production I made in the Belasco Theatre, for the reason that the nature of its dedicatory play, "The Grand Army Man," did not demand such treatment. But a large part of "The Return of Peter Grimm" was acted without footlights because that play required these methods for perfect illusion and artistic effect. And footlights were not in use at all in "Marie-Odile," nor was their use contemplated at any time while the production was being prepared. Its immediate predecessor, "The Phantom Rival," by Ferenc Molnar, the Hungarian dramatist, was produced according to the same methods, as far as lighting is concerned. Entire scenes of the dream play might have been unsuccessful in an artistic sense if I had resorted to the common lighting methods for producing its hazy dream effects.

I might have turned into a means for publicity my footlight device, and many others, either originated by myself, invented by my mechanical experts, or borrowed from theatres of the distant past, but it has never occurred to me to do so. I even have certain appliances by which I am able to install my own lighting process temporarily in theatres outside of New York, when my companies are on tour.

I fear I have been rather too tolerant of the attacks by many of our writers on the subject of dramatic art, whose eyes are fixed on the foreign stage and to whom it never seems to occur that our native accomplishments in the theatre are entitled to recognition and encouragement.

A few years ago I became convinced that the use of orchestras and entr'acte music in the theatre was often destructive to the illusion of what was taking place on the stage and calculated to interfere with the imaginative quality which I was attempting to put into my productions. In other words, I came to believe that an orchestra, however delightful its music, produced a discordant note in the theatre.

Therefore I resolved to do away with my orchestra altogether. I dismissed my musicians and concealed my orchestra pit beneath a canopy of flowers. I signaled the raising of the curtain by means of subdued and beautifully modulated chimes.

I confess that I was astounded when some of the critics with supposedly clear perceptions and knowledge of the theatre and dramatic art immediately proclaimed that, in the interest of economy, David Belasco was depriving his patrons of the luxury of music in his theatres, or that, owing to the drastic demands of the musical unions, David Belasco had become so exasperated that he had driven his musicians out of his theatres. Since that time about half the theatres in New York, where legitimate dramas are acted, have followed my view and dispensed altogether with music.

There has been progress, too apparent to be mistakable, in the art of playwriting. Our dramatists, as generation has succeeded generation, are viewing life with a clearer vision. The art of the theatre has not moved backward; it grows constantly more faithful to the conditions which it aims to depict, preserving always the best usages of the past. The theatre is drawing nearer to nature. The images reflected by its mirror are ever more authentic. The theatre is more and more, and ever more, dedicated to the service of beauty and truth. Its art is being constantly refined in the crucible of experience. There will always be plenty of theatres where the appeal from the stage will be to the healthy imagination and the normal mind, and among these theatres will be mine.

THE END

Date Due

APR 5 78			

Demco 38-297